In the First and Second Editions pul
'Guide to Sark' carried advertisem
editors thought it would be fitting t
advertisers to try to match the 'tone
their own. We are very grateful to:

CW00879764

La Sablonnerie Hotel, The
Guille, Small Island Publ
who took up the invitation to adver.   ie
charming advertisements. We hope our readers will support them in return.

All of the fees generated were paid directly to the Professor Saint Medical Trust.

Immediately on landing in SARK
do not fail to pay a visit to ———

JOHN PHILIP de CARTERET

Grocer, Tea Dealer and Provision
Merchant, Avenue House, Sark.
OPPOSITE BEL - AIR HOTEL

A Large Selection of Sark Stone Brooches, Hat Pins and Crested Goss China always on sale

AFTERNOON TEAS SUPPLIED

PH. DE CARTERET	Johannes' Eau de Cologne
Near the Church	(Qualité Superfine)
SARK	J. W. JONES, 28 Arcade
PEACHES &c. fresh daily	Guernsey

The Noted House for Pound Cake, Lemon Sponge Cake
and Biscuits.
GUERNSEY GACHE THE SPECIALITY.
13 & 14, Vauvert Street, Guernsey. Telephone 468.
Proprietor : L. A. LE HURAY.

Guernsey Entertainments & Visitors' Guide

Post free, on application, to all parts of the United Kingdom

Address—Publisher, 10, Smith Street, Guernsey

EXPERIENCE SARK AS PART OF OVER *400 YEARS* OF UNBROKEN HISTORY WITH THE **GUILLE FAMILY**, DIRECT DESCENDENTS OF ONE OF THE ORIGINAL TENEMENT HOLDERS.

George Guille

Experience the 'Round the Island' boat trip (see Route 21) with a highly experienced boatman, who knows every inch of the coastline, in his famous boat, the **'Non Pareil'**.

- See the **caves** and places **difficult or impossible** to get to by land.
- Experience sea-life at close quarters, and the best chance of seeing **dolphins, puffins** and other sea-birds, dependent on season.

Sue Guille

- **Luxury**, en-suite, Bed and Breakfast accommodation.
- **Fresh, home cooked food**, with home-made preserves at breakfast.
- **Highly recommended** by the gentlefolk of **Tripadvisor**.

For both, contact: Sue Guille, Cae de Mat, Sark, GY1 0SA

Tel: 00 44 (0)1481 832107.   **e mail** sueguille@hotmail.com

Frontispiece
The ravages of time: the engine house of the Sark Hope Silver Mine pictured (a) in the time of the Latrobe brothers' Guide to Sark in 1914, (b) as it has looked for the past 50 years and (c) following the Valentine's Day gale in 2014, illustrating the relative transience of man's interference with Sark, faced with time and the elements. Will brambles have reclaimed it completely in another 50 years?

A REVISED AND ENLARGED

La Trobe

GUIDE TO SARK

Containing a detailed description of

THE COAST, CAVES AND BAYS

G. & L. LATROBE
Originally Published 1914

This Centenary Edition
2014
Lazarus Publications N.F.P.

'The La Trobe Guide to the Coast, Caves and Bays of Sark'
Completely Revised 7th (Centenary) Edition.
Published: 2014

Published by: Lazarus Publications NFP,
Newmarket,
Suffolk, CB8 8RD,
UK.
E mail:lazarusnfp@btinternet.com

First Published as:
'Guide to Sark'
G and L Latrobe
by Tozers Printers, Guernsey, 1914

This edition based on the 6th Edition, published by Guernsey Press Co. LTD,
1980, no copyright declared.

Foreword to the 1964 6th Edition

'The "Latrobe" Guide has been out of print for many years; its absence has been frequently deplored, and it is in answer to repeated requests that this revised and enlarged edition has been published.

Much has happened in the interim; many alterations, omissions and corrections have perforce been made, but the Publishers have endeavoured to keep to the spirit of the "Latrobes" who were, before all else, enthusiasts for Sark; it is hoped that another generation will come to appreciate them no less than their predecessors.'

A.G.P. 1964.

The present editors cannot express their view more succinctly and clearly than this past one. We have tried to achieve exactly the same result, to exactly the same purpose.
We hope we have succeeded.
We are indebted to the efforts of all those who have gone before us in keeping this wonderful guide in print for most of 100 years.

Jeremy la Trobe-Bateman and Rob Pilsworth, 2014

Foreword to the 2014 Centenary Edition

I was delighted when I heard that the 'La Trobe Guide' was to be up-dated and republished. The original was the 'must have' guide for all those who enjoy scrambling round the cliffs and foreshore of Sark, to find all the hidden joys unseen by the average visitor and dare I say it by many locals as well.

Over the years the Guide has been revised many times, most recently in 1994. Since then, there have been many small - and one or two large - changes to the landscape due to land erosion and change of paths, making any thought of a simple upgrade impracticable. The guide is now completely revised but retains the original aim of making the entire Island more accessible to locals and visitor alike, whilst retaining the original charm. I have no reservation in recommending this guide to all who wish to explore and enjoy Sark to the full.

J.M.Beaumont, OBE, Seigneur of Sark, 2014

CONTENTS

PREFACE TO FIRST EDITION.

INTRODUCTION, containing —

        Historical Note.

        Why go to Sark?

        The Approach — a General Description.

        Recommendations for Day Visitors.

        Fishing.

        Hints and Cautions.

THE CHANNEL AND FRENCH COAST.

THE COAST DESCRIBED: Walks, Bathes, Scrambles, Caves, Fishing, etc.

MAP OF SARK.

PREFACE
To the First Edition

THE Island of Sark, although of considerable antiquity, from an historian's point of view, has not until some years ago become well known from a visitor's standpoint

The object of this Guide is to assist all varieties of visitors to the island. First, and certainly not least, the many who come over from Guernsey and sometimes Jersey, for the day only.

It is attempted in this Guide to show these visitors what can be accomplished in the five or six hours allowed between the arrival and departure of their steamer, and how this time can be filled in to the best possible enjoyment, allowing ample time for lunch at one of the various places in the island, having also due regard to the tides, which are most important factors for seeing the many caves and rock scenery.

Secondly, for those visitors who are more fortunate and have the opportunity of a longer visit to the island, further and fuller information is given.

Should visitors follow these routes in order and in detail they will find that a second visit to Sark can be still further enjoyed and that the beauties of the island grow year by year; indeed, those who have been there many years never acknowledge they are tired of it, nor that they even know it thoroughly.

The authors have therefore attempted to compile this work in a kind of sequence, which can be followed by all visitors easily, both by letterpress and maps.

To all of these the unique beauties of the island must appeal, the rugged sea line, its sea views and caves, its ever changing colours in heather, gorse and flowers, the beautiful colours and contours of its rocks, whether at morning, noon, or night, its wonderful sunsets, and ever varying sea tints.

Truly a wonderful little island that lies so near our homes and, as yet, so little known.

The authors and publishers will welcome any suggestions or ideas from readers which will be of great value and assistance in future editions.

THE LATROBES.

Sark, July, 1914.

[Where descriptions of places have become factually incorrect, changes have been made to the original text. Where new information has come to light since the original publication of this book, it has been added by the current editors in bracketed italics-J.L.T-B. and R.P. 2014]

INTRODUCTION

1.—*Historical Note.*

The first records we have of Sark, extant, appear about the sixth century, when a monastery was founded by Saint Maglorious, on the site on which La Moinerie now in all probability stands.

However, it seems probable, from the existence of druidical and other ancient relics, that Sark under the name of Sargia was at one time occupied by the Romans. *[Recent excavations by Sir Barry Cunnliffe and a team from Oxford University show occupation intermittently since the stone age, some 7,000 yrs ago].* Some time later Sark, with the other Islands, was annexed by the Normans, and through that influence was attached in the thirteenth century to the English Crown

In the next century all these former traces of civilisation appear to have vanished and the Island became deserted. Indeed, up to the middle of the sixteenth century no permanent inhabitants seem to have occupied Sark, but it was used as a headquarters by various piratical chieftains.

From these pests the Island was purged by the English Fleet in the time of Edward VI, but in 1549 it was seized by the French, and occupied by 400 soldiers under Captain Bruel.

This garrison only held Sark for six years, during which time three forts were built, visible today at the Eperquerie, in Little Sark near La Coupee and above Derrible Bay.

The reign of Queen Elizabeth was an important one both for Jersey, governed at the time by Sir Walter Raleigh, and still more so for Sark.

As the Island had again become completely deserted, the Queen appointed Helier de Carteret as seigneur, thus establishing the regime that has lasted, to all intents and purposes, to the present day.

The Seigneur was given many peculiar rights, so that in the Island he became supreme; the great Queen knew well that a few honours carefully given went a long way.

A piece of cannon presented to the first Seigneur by Queen Elizabeth I, can still be seen in the Seigneurie grounds. Helier de Carteret brought with him forty families to colonise the Island, and the land was divided among them on a species of feudal tenure, which greatly conduced to the improved cultivation of the Island.

9

The Island remained in the hands of the De Carterets until the death of Sir Charles de Carteret, Bart., who died without issue in 1715.

Under his will the property was sold and passed through the hands of James Milner and the Bishop of Gloucester into the keeping of the Le Pelley family, which supplied eight successive Seigneurs of Sark.

During this period many improvements were introduced, but through the disastrous results of the silver mines, which were started in 1835, Peter Le Pelley was forced to sell the property in 1852, when the present family purchased it.

For constitutional, political, legal, and ecclesiastical purposes Sark is still in the Bailiwick of Guernsey. Yet it has a Court of its own, which consists of Seneschal (or judge), Prevot (or sheriff), and the Greffier (registrar), who, together with the President and elected members, constitute the Court of Chief Pleas of Sark.

2.—*Why go to Sark?*

In these days of mass motoring and "package" holidays a place which bans the motor car and abjures the holiday camp needs little advertisement, especially if it has a high sunshine average, beauty, peace and space.

When the Latrobe's Guide was first published the journey from Guernsey to London took nearly ten hours longer than it does today. Although the passage from Guernsey to Sark has been accelerated by the use of high powered launches, the basic service vessel still takes about the same time as did its predecessors at the turn of the century.

Therefore, the reasons for visiting Sark proffered by the La Trobes — which we print beneath un-amended — seem to have even greater force today than when they were set down in 1914:

"It might well strike a stranger, that to pay a visit to Sark, which is such an out-of-the-way spot, must be rather foolish and dull: how could it bear comparison with any of the better known holiday resorts?

It will be convenient, therefore, to detail the various attractions of the Island at some length

The surest evidence that such attractions exist, and greatly so, is afforded by the fact that once a visit has been paid to Sark, the visitor always longs to repeat in following years the happy weeks of his previous holiday in the "Pearl of Islands".

Moreover, not only are the charms of the Island very great, but they are extremely varied, so as to suit people of all tastes and proclivities.

In the first place, there is that fascinating old-world feeling in Sark that many visitors find so interesting: Sark with its feudal constitution and ancient rights is, as it were, a relic of an almost forgotten past. *[Some of these remain, some have been abolished to satisfy modern thinking]*.

The curious customs, the native patois *(now very rarely spoken)*, the kindliness and good feeling of the people all have a great charm of their own to those who come to Sark tired and out of sorts from their work.

Then Sark is the utopia of those who require nothing but rest and quiet; it is hard to imagine a better rest cure than to spend an idle day or week lying on the bracken-covered slopes, amid the bracing air, while the low murmur of the sea on the rocks far below soothes the senses, while on all sides there is a wild profusion of flowers of all descriptions.

In May, June and July especially the wild flowers are superb each corner revealing new and unexpected beauties; while in the Autumn the ferns become golden, and the hills in the evening sun are a mass of gold and purple.

But it must not be imagined that there is nothing to do in Sark but to sit idle.

For those who are energetically inclined there is an inexhaustible mine of interest to be laid open to their gaze.

Sark, with all its coastline of forty miles, always holds in reserve new secrets, even from those who imagine they know it well.

The bathing, the rocks, the pools, and the climbing are so varied and charming that the visitor is at first almost bewildered in the midst of so great a profusion of delights.

Here, too, Sark holds out her hands to all sorts and conditions of people.

For there is bathing, and rocks, and pools for those unable or undesirous of much exercise or of hard climbing as well as for those who are ready and eager to climb and clamber over every headland, and pry into the secrets of every bay.

There are many places where the descents to the sea are quite simple, and in the majority of places there is shallow bathing for those who cannot swim, close to the deep-water plunge for those who can.

Finally there is fishing, from headland or from boat, and those interested in this sport will find plenty of scope in this direction.

But perhaps the chief charm of the island, greater than, or rather allied with, its beauty, its air, and its position, is the fascination of discovering new and unknown spots on the coast.

The real lover of Sark is never content until he thinks he has been everywhere it is possible to go, until he knows every pool, and every headland; and even on his next visit it is almost inevitable that still further secrets will be revealed to him, proving that to know Sark thoroughly would take a lifetime of holidays.

Anyhow seeing is believing, so come to Sark and see.

3.—The approach to Sark (a general description).

When first viewed as the boat leaves Guernsey Harbour, Sark appears to be a small, precipitous and uninhabited rock. The visitor quickly finds how erroneous that impression is.

There are, it is true, hardly any houses visible from the sea, all of them, as far as possible, being situated in protected nooks and glens—the winter winds of Sark are an experience which the summer visitor cannot imagine.

The actual size of the Island is 3½ miles in length from the Bec du Nez in the North to Port Gorey in the South; and 1½ miles in its broadest part, from Creux Harbour to the Gouliot Caves.

It is divided into two distinct portions—Big Sark and Little Sark, joined by a natural causeway more than 100 yards (100 m.) long and 320 ft. (92 m.) above sea level, called La Coupee. This narrow way is one of the sights of the Channel Islands, and its position can be clearly seen from the boat, where the skyline of the Island towards the south drops sharply for a short distance and abruptly rises again.

The area of Sark is barely 1,300 English acres. It lies 7 miles E.S.E. of Guernsey, and the distance from port to port is 9 miles. The highest point on the Island is at the Windmill, 375 feet (about 110 m.) above sea level, and here on a fine day all the Channel Islands and the coast of France may be seen. The population at the last census was 560. - 800 ?

The boat usually approaches Sark by the northern passage, hugging the island of Jethou and affording a good view of Herm, and then as it heads towards the Bec du Nez one can bit by bit pick out the outstanding features as the boat threads its way through the dangerous and half submerged rocks. First the Mill, then the Pilcher Monument and the Island of Brechou divided from Sark by the Gouliot Passage, familiar to filmgoers in the 1951 film, *"Appointment with Venus"*. Then one by one the various headlands and bays reveal themselves until the boat passes within a stone's throw of the weather beaten rocks at the north of the Island, pitching and rolling in the bubbling tide. Once round the point, calmer water is usually encountered and one is at liberty to examine the eastern coast and the rocks lying off it. First, La Pecheresse off the Eperquerie Landing, then the Petit and Grand Moies and finally Point Robert and the Lighthouse, with the Dog Cave lying almost immediately beneath.

The brief glimpse one gains as the boat passes the wide and inviting bays, enormous caves and grim headlands merely serves to whet the appetite for inspecting them personally.

If one is lucky enough to make the journey in May or early June when the cliffs are aflame with colour and all Sark is a rock garden, the sight, and smell, too, will remain a permanent recollection.

Rounding Point Robert the Maseline Harbour is at once in view with the waiting tractors with their luggage trailers and all the bustle of reception.

The romantic old harbour at "Le Creux" round the next headland, is nowadays seldom used unless wind prohibits a landing at Maseline.

Once ashore labeled luggage can be left to the carters, and will invariably find the visitor eventually! Ascent to the top of the island is by a tractor drawn 'bus' (the 'toast-rack') or an uphill walk of some twenty minutes until the Plateau of Sark, some 350 feet (about 100 m.) above sea level, is reached by a footpath through a wooded valley by a stream, which runs alongside a winding picturesque road, while on both sides the hills slope gradually upwards clothed in bracken and their brilliant seasonal bloom, until, at last, the Bel Air Inn and the Collinette crossroads are reached.

It is here that the day visitor must decide what he wishes to see, for to go everywhere is impossible. To help in this decision various suggestions are made on Page 16. It is around here, too, that such merchandise as the Island stocks can be purchased, bicycles can he hired and refreshments taken. The principal hotels provide luncheon and there are several cafes and tea houses.

These crossroads a La Collinette form the base from which most of the Routes in this Guide commence, and any distances and timings are given from them. One of the roads is that by which the visitor has just ascended from the Harbour, and its direct continuation is known as The Avenue. The road to the left past the National Westminster Bank leads to Derrible Bay, the Hogs Back and Dixcart Bay, while the remaining road, known as Rue Lucas, leads to the northern part of the Island.

Taking them in turn, the left hand ways to the Derribles, the Hogs Back and Dixcart Bay are fully described under Routes 6, 7 and 8.

The Avenue leads to the Post Office and then breaks left to the Prison, the former Girls' School *(now the Visitor Tourist Information Centre, and home to the display of the Societe Serquaise)* and finally into the Rue du Moulin, where a footpath to Stocks and Dixcart Hotels is signposted. The fork to the right leads to the Vicarage and Church, the obsolete Island Hall and former Boys' School, in which latter the Chief Pleas holds its meetings. The Church, built in 1820, contains some tablets of interest, and is worth a visit. It stands in the very centre of Sark. *(The former Boys and Girls Schools have now been replaced, along with the obsolete Island Hall, by a magnificent new school and hall complex, with a bar and restaurant, on the road to the Seigneurie Gardens).*

With the exception of royalty and sea birds, the journey to Sark has always been over the sea. This is pictured over the years with the arrival into the old harbour of (a) the 'Courier' in the 1930's, (b) the 'Fleet Commodore' in the 1960's and (c) the current main tourist vessel the 'Sark Belle', with an unofficial ships-pilot, superbly photographed by Sue Daly in the dolphin summer of 2014.

Plate I

(a)

(b)

(c)

For centuries travel from the harbours to the top of the island was on foot or by horse-drawn carriage only (a). This changed in the 1970's when increased visitor numbers, congestion at the quayside, and concern for the hardworking horses prompted a change. The transport of visitors from the quayside to the top of the island plateau is now achieved with the use of a tractor-drawn bus (b), affectionately nicknamed 'The Toast-rack'. Once at the top of the hill passengers alight, and continue their journey in horse-drawn carriages (c).

Plate II

The fourth and last road from Collinette—Rue Lucas—leads northward, a right hand road goes to the Mermaid Inn and the Lighthouse while at the first crossroads—Le Carrefour--a turn to the right leads to La Ville Roussel, La Greve de la Ville, etc., while that to the left goes to the former Boys' School and the Rue du Sermon at the Clos a Jaon crossroads.

Proceeding straight ahead from Le Carrefour, we pass several houses, bending left at Le Fort to form a junction with the Clos Jaon-Seigneurie Road at a point within easy reach of Eperquerie Common (see Route 1).

Turning south along the Clos Jaon road, we pass the turning to Port du Moulin on the right (see Route 18) and the Seigneurie, where, by kind permission, the Gardens are opened to visitors daily.

Turning right along the Rue du Sermon, the Methodist Chapel and old Graveyard are reached at another road junction. The rough road forward is a cul de sac leading to Port a la Jument, while on the left hand is the main road leading to La Coupee and Little Sark, joining the Rue du Moulin at the Vaurocque crossroads a short distance ahead. Here the right hand turn leads to the Beauregard Hotel *[now demolished by the new owners]* and Hotel Petit Champs, the Pilcher Monument, Havre Gosselin and Gouliot caves. While the left hand turn leads back to the Avenue, passing the old Sark Windmill and rejoining the Avenue at the former Girls' School and Prison *[now the Sark Tourist Information Centre, and home to the display of the Societe de Serquaise, open to the public]*.

Straight ahead from the Vaurocque crossroad, the Coupee is a good ten minutes' walk, and La Sablonnerie Hotel on Little Sark as much again.

EXCURSIONS SUITABLE FOR DAY VISITORS

A list of excursions, any of which are suitable for a day's visit, together with approximate times and distances from La Collinette, which is adopted as the base, is given beneath.

La Collinette to:

La Maseline Harbour	20 minutes	See Route 5
The Eperquerie Landing	30 minutes	See Route 1
Derrible Bay	35 minutes	See Route 6
Dixcart bay	30 minutes	See Route 8
La Coupee	30 minutes	See Route 15
Venus' Bath	60 minutes	See Route 11
Pilcher Monument	20 minutes	See Route 16
Gouliot Caves	45 minutes	See Route 17
Port d Moulin	45 minutes	See Route 18
Greve de la Ville	30 minutes	See Route 4
La Seigneurie Gardens	15 minutes	See Route 18

In many cases it takes longer to come up than go down and the approximate times given allow for the former event.

Fishing. It is occasionally possible to get a day's deep sea fishing, but the boats are not numerous, and special arrangements must be made. Most common fish are mackerel, pollack, whiting and conger.

Threadline fishing from the rocks is becoming popular and suggested stations are marked with an F on the Sketch Plans, the most popular being the Harbours Maseline and Creux, the Eperquerie, La Congriere and Havre Gosselin. Principal takings are Bass, Pollack, Grey Mullet, Mackerel and Rock Fish. Quantities of lobster and crab are caught in season.

4.—Some useful Hints and Cautions.

Walking. It is well known that there are no motor cars on Sark, but townspeople and motorists do not always realise that there is much walking or cycling to be done, that Sark coastwise is not a small island, and that there is no public transport, or indeed, any transport to bring tired families home. Therefore, come prepared for walking; bicycles can be hired.

Outings. Visitors find it most convenient to take a packed lunch, which hotels and guest-houses most willingly provide. Rucksacks are therefore a useful provision, and pneumatic cushions can be a comfort for the sedentary. One of the conveniences of an island is being able to elude any wind. Sark has charming resorts at all points of the compass, a study of the weather vane before setting out is rewarding. The sun's rays are very strong in Sark, and severe cases of over-exposure are not uncommon.

Bathing. The bathing in Sark is very good, some hold, the finest in Western waters. It is also generally very safe. Off the rocks the water is deep and crystal clear, and if on a first occasion it feels a little cold, the tonic effect is remarkable. Good beaches and rock bathes are marked with a B on the Sketch Plans. As a general rule rock bathing is best at half tide up. It is unwise to bathe off the end of promontories or in obvious currents.

Tides. The Bay of Mont St. Michel has one of the greatest tide movements in the world and for this reason the tides and currents around Sark are important to note if any attempt at really seeing the coast and caves is to be made. They are extremely dangerous and great care must be exercised. The rise and fall is so considerable that the whole coast of the Island alters its aspect in the process.

At the fortnightly spring tides the rise and fall is said to exceed 10 metres, whereas during the neap tides in alternate weeks it is but 6 metres. As several of the best caves can only be visited during a spring tide, it is most important to note when these occur. As there is some doubt as to the actual tide range in Sark (the Guernsey facing coast is said to vary from the Jersey and French facing coast) the recommendations in this Guide are based on the Tide Tables produced by Guernsey marine businesses and available free at the Gallery Stores, which give an excellent summary of spring tides. No one who intends to visit the remoter parts of the island should be without a copy.

Occasionally, about four times a year, extra large tides occur called Grand Marees, when the rise and fall is about 2 feet over normal spring tide range.

The currents are strongest at the north of the Island, off Creux Harbour, between L'Etac and Little Sark, and in the Gouliot Pass. However, round the headlands there is a dangerous current and the wise swimmer will not venture too far out from the shore. These latter can only be learnt by experience.

The various directions of the currents are as follows:

From Creux Harbour right away to L'Etac and Little Sark the stream runs 7½ hours to the eastward, but only 4½ to the south-west. The eastward stream beginning an hour after low water and the south-west at 2½ hours ebb.

From the Bec du Nez along the north-west coast, the tide starts to run southward at three-quarter flood along the land until the force of the Gouliot stream turns it north-westward again. The north-easterly stream sets in at three-quarter ebb, through Herm, the stream runs for equal time, setting in northward at half flood and reversing at half ebb.

On the south-western coast of Sark the stream runs northward at half flood for one hour, then suddenly reversing runs south-westward for 11 hours, then half-an-hour before high water on the rocks it turns northwards until half ebb.

Lastly, from Bec du Nez to Creux Harbour, the stream runs 8½ hours south-east and 3½ hours north-west, starting southward at four hours flood and then setting back northward for the remainder.

Note that as the northward stream continues twice as long as the southward stream, the latter has to flow with far greater strength to make up for time and the former is always slack.

N.B. The recommended footages necessary to reach caves, etc. are given in this Guide as a rough indication, it must always be borne in mind that wind and barometric pressure can substantially affect the tide range.

Footpaths. There are many footpaths in Sark, and **no rights of way.** The ways to most bays and beaches, except to landing places, are by courtesy of the owners of the land. So long as visitors display good manners and a due regard for livestock, no objection to their passage is likely.

On the Sketch Plans, ways which are customarily used are indicated with the word "path". Where there is no easily distinguishable track, the words "way up" are used. But it must be emphasised that these do not constitute any public rights, and if in doubt, permission should be asked. Sark people are extremely courteous and a rebuff is most unlikely.

Scrambling. Some of the Routes in this book cover sections of the coast which require a low tide and expenditure of some energy to accomplish if as much as possible of the Island is to be visited. None are impossible to able-bodied persons, but some require a little more skill and care than others. The reader, therefore, must not be put off when a scramble is described as "difficult" or "very difficult", the phrase merely signifying that a greater degree of care than usual should be exercised. In the majority of cases the worst that can befall is a ducking.

Otherwise these coastal excursions are best described as, at the most, arduous, scrambles from point to point and the sole requirements are rope-soled shoes *[or walking boots]* for slippery rocks, rucksacks to free the hands, and torches for the caves. Scrambling in bathing costumes is uncomfortable and unnecessary. All the same, it is unwise to go scrambling alone, an ankle can be sprained and some obstacles need help in negotiation.

The tides turn very quickly on this Island, so a close watch should always be kept on the time, ensuring adequate time for a safe return

Sketch Plans. Needless to say, the Sketch Plans are not to scale, the suggested routes are indicated by a dotted or solid line, and 'Path' where applicable.

THE CHANNEL AND THE FRENCH COAST

Jersey, Guernsey, Alderney and Sark; who does not recollect this, merely as an old tag learnt at school, or even before those days. The first three generally being regarded as the home of various breeds of cows and the latter either disregarded altogether or thought of as a bleak, bare, storm-swept rock.

So are the Channel Islands regarded by a great many others who have been to Jersey and Guernsey and only know Sark from a five-hour day visit, and dismiss it with the non-committal phrase, "Oh! a nice little place," and these people "do" Sark in five hours.

Lastly, there are those who have stayed in Sark year after year; for there are few who have stayed there for a holiday in one year only — they always come back.

What better proof have we, or can we desire, than these repeated visits, and these people know that so far from "doing" Sark in five hours they have not been able to do it thoroughly in five or ten years.

A visitor to Sark naturally likes to know his surroundings, so as to be able to take intelligent interest in what he sees around him, and the best places to see the surrounding Islands from are the Mill or the Pilcher Monument above Havre Gosselin.

From the Mill in the evenings the best view of the neighbouring lighthouses can be obtained (See map page 4).

Lights to be seen from Old Mill, Sark, on a clear night:

		Miles
St. Martin's Point	Three flashes every 10 sec.	7 W.
St, Peter Port (Breakwater)	Alternate white and red	7 W.N.W.
Platte Fougere	Flash every 10 secs.	7 N.W.
Casquets	Five flashes every 30 secs.	17 N.W.
Quenard Point (Alderney]	Four flashes every 15 secs.	20 N.
Cap de la la Hague	Flash every 5 secs.	23 E.N.E.
Carteret (France)	Three flashes every 15 secs.	22 E.S.E.
Grosnez (Jersey)	Two flashes every 15 secs.	11 S.S. E.
Corbiere (Jersey)	Occurring every 10 secs.	16 S.
Roches Douvres (France)	Flash every 5 secs.	26 W.S.W

SKETCH PLAN No 1

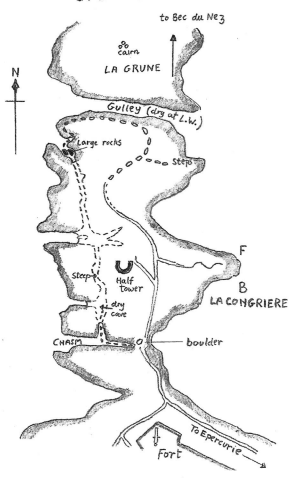

THE NORTH OF THE ISLAND
and
BOUTIQUES CAVES

A day can be happily spent on this promontory—good bathing at all tides around the Eperquerie Landing where there is also a shallow pool for children. At half tide up, good deep bathing at Congriere (B on plan) and also in the sea entrance to the Boutique Caves, the descent to the latter needs some care. Fishermen favour the Congriere — the rocks adjacent to the Eperquerie Landing are also popular (F on plan). For the more energetic the Boutique Caves can be explored on any low tide and a rock scrambling visit may be paid to the northern tip of Sark — the Bec du Nez. The Eperquerie Common is ideal for picnics and affords a splendid view of the Islands of the Bailiwick of Guernsey and of the coast of France.

Take the road from Collinette leading north and go straight up the Rue Lucas and Route du Fort, at the Fort turn to the left and then at the road junction turn right; after 200 m the road ends at a turning-area where cycles may be left.

A winding cart track leads across the Common to the Eperquerie Landing where we find good rocks for bathing or lunching and a paddling pool for children. *[The first part of this cart track is usually missed by taking the narrow footpath just through the hedge from the road as a short-cut].*

Those who wish to visit the Boutique Caves should leave the Eperquerie Landing an hour or so before low tide and take the path up to the first cannon overlooking the pool and then instead of following the cart track, take the path on the edge of the cliff leading outside the wall, going northwards.

Continue along here until just before the half-round tower on the hill *[a former shelter for the target-setter during musket practice in the 18th century]*— a gulley leading down to the beach will be seen. The top of the gulley juts into the path slightly and beside it there is a great boulder, beneath which unnecessary impedimenta may be left; descend this gulley or chasm, keeping as soon as practicable to the right hand side. About half way down, another narrow chasm opens upwards to the right and at the top a hole in the cliff face can be seen; this is the 'chimney' entrance to the "Boutiques" and having ascended and passed over a sill, we find ourselves in a dry cave the floor of which, having been formed by roof-fall, comprises the only dry area in which contraband could have been stored. Move swiftly through (the roof is very fragile!) and pass the silted up sea entrance on the left of this chamber, climb steeply down over the large rocks where it is quite dark and there is a pool, and a squeeze through a narrow aperture leading to the main sea cave.

Two caves on the right continue some little distance inland. Having explored them, take the entrance immediately facing the one by which the sea cave was reached, this cave is a long dark tunnel and at one point the roof falls suddenly, there are also one or two shallow pools; the exit is blocked by two large black rocks, but they can be passed without much difficulty. Cross the gully to the left and ascend around the end of the headland to reach the path.

Those who wish to scramble along to the north end of Sark should descend from this path to the gulley dividing La Grune from the main island, by way of some concrete steps and a scramble. Keeping to the right of the following islands the Bec du Nez can be reached easily. Bathing here is dangerous on account of the strong tide and an eye should be kept on the gulley between La Grune and the main Island as it fills quickly on a rising tide and becomes dangerous to cross.

Having re-crossed it, the way back is easy. Keeping the half-round tower to our right the point of original descent is soon reached, and the homeward journey is made by the former route.

(The caves are now normally taken in reverse (N to S directions) as ascending the slopes is less "hair-raising".)

SKETCH PLAN No. 2

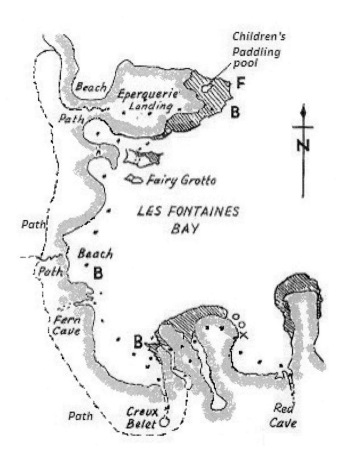

Children's Paddling pool

F

Beach

Eperquerie Landing

B

Path

N

Fairy Grotto

LES FONTAINES BAY

Path

Path

Beach

B

Path

Fern Cave

B

Path

Creux Belet

Red Cave

24

LES FONTAINES BAY
EPERQUERIE TO THE RED CAVE

**(This Bay must not be confused with the equally
delightful Fontaines Bay and Creek in Little Sark,
see Routes 13 and 14)**

For those who prefer to spend a lazy day on the beach where bathing is good except at low tide, the best means of approach is to take the path leading off the track to Eperquerie Landing (see Route 1). It branches to the right just before an old metal rail bizarrely planted upright by the road, and descends a charming valley. At the bottom, paths branch to the right to reach the Creux Belet, and left to join the Eperquerie landing path. The path to Les Fontaines beach is straight ahead. (see Sketch Plan 2)

Rock scramblers should proceed to the Eperquerie Landing (Route 1).

The scramble from Eperquerie to the Creux Belet is interesting, easy and can be made on any low tide — the extension to the Red Cave is dealt with later.

Descend the rocks to the south of the children's pool at Eperquerie—see Route 1, follow the coast a short way until a natural arch can be seen across a small inlet. It is detached from the cliff and a closer inspection reveals another similarly isolated arch behind. This delightful piece of rock scenery was named The Fairy Grotto by William Toplis, R.A., whose painting is well-known. The shape of the distant arch resembles the figure of a woman in trailing draperies, an illusion which is effective when the sun is directly overhead.

We must now retrace our steps to view the cove which stands at the head of this little inlet and find our way on through a tunnel which leads through the cliff to Les Fontaines Bay where there is a path up to the Eperquerie Common and a good beach for bathing.

A little beyond the steps up to the path will be found The Fern Cave, also named by William Toplis after a painting. The ferns are not prolific now but the cavern exposes some fine rock colouring.

Crossing the seaweed southwards we pass two small caves of no consequence to approach the Creux Belet, interesting, because it is too far above the tide level to allow a scouring of the fallen debris and thus enables a close examination to be made of the formation — it is not, however, a very dramatic feature, the height of the shaft is not great and can easily be approach from above. The way up is via the rock reef lying alongside the cave, at its seaward end, and, once on the slab, a rope hanging down assist us onto the path. The easiest way home perhaps is to return to the path by the Fern Cave in Fontaine Bay, rejoining Route 1 at Eperquerie Common.

These rocks and creeks at Creux Belet are a good bathing place for a small party at the top of the tide.

Extension to the Red Cave.

This interesting little scramble can only be attempted on a good spring tide falling to 1.1 m. or less, the difficult parts are climbing out of the Creux Belet creek and at the point marked X on the Sketch Plan where dead low water is needed - here descent must be made to the Red Cave or Drinking Horse Cave. No time should be lost as the tolerance is no more than half-an-hour. It lies right under the adjacent headland; two small caves just before it are negligible. Apart from the little difficulty above described, the scramble is extremely interesting: it includes two fine collapsed Creux and the Red Cave itself, with its central column resembling a drinking horse is one of the most interesting in the Island.

The tide rises fast here and unless a wetting is to be incurred, the return to Creux Belet should he made good without delay as although there is a way up round the next headland, it should not be attempted without a guide.

(a)

(b)

A typical 'Sark scramble' (a) taken from the 1960's Fourth Edition, and the man-made 'boat-wedge' mooring (b) created at the Banquette landing which makes for a perfect gradually descending slope into the sea for swimming.

Plate III

(a)

(b)

The view from the lighthouse in the 1930s, with the steamer heading towards Guernsey (a) and, Fontaine Bay-just around the corner from the Eperquerie landing (b).

Plate IV

THE BANQUETTE

Easy descent — Excellent deep-water Bathing at all tides.

To reach the Banquette Landing, take the route to The Fort. Go past the cottages, towards the canon, and there is a high wooden fence and a signed gate to the right, with an open fronted workshop straight ahead. Go through (or around) the gate, and walk across the paddock to the edge of a wire-fenced enclosure. Keep this on your right, and walk to a small gap in a raised bank. Through this, the steps down to the woodland path can be seen. This gorge is a splendid place to see the spring flowers.

The Banquette rocks are flat and make a good place for lunch and the afternoon sun stays later here than almost anywhere else on this coast of Sark; the bathing is first-class for those who can swim, but no good for others as the rocks are surrounded by deep water. It is a popular place with skin-divers.The view is magnificent. Southwards, on the right, the green slopes rise sharply to the sky, while on the left the sea idly laps the wild-looking rocks of the Grand and Petit Moies; straight ahead is La Greve de la Ville with its cliffs and caves and away on the horizon the rim of France dips to the saltings south of Carteret.

The "Landing" has but one drawback — size: perfect for one party and barely sufficient for two. Late comers are advised to break away from the path where it takes its final dip to the rocks and work along the cliff northwards, keeping as low as possible. Several excellent gullics and creeks will be discovered where the bathing is equally good and peace is more possessive.

This coast is seldom explored and is very interesting. Given reasonable care there are several places where a descent on to the rocks can easily be made. The one disadvantage being that the afternoon sun does not stay so long here as at the "Landing" itself.

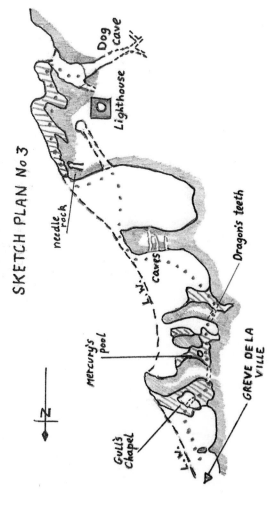

SKETCH PLAN No 3

N

Dog Cave

Lighthouse

needle rock

Mercury's Pool

Gull's Chapel

L.W.

Caves

Dragon's teeth

L.W.

GREVE DE LA VILLE

28

LA GREVE DE LA VILLE

**Easy descent—popular beach Bathe — easy and
interesting Scramble through the Gull's Chapel
Caves with an extension to The Dog Cave on a
grand maree.**

From the Collinette, take Rue Lucas as in Route l as far as the first cross-roads (Le Carrefour), turn right to La Ville Roussell and at T right-handed again, following the road round until a little common is reached, with a path round the edge which leads to the entrance to the path down the side of a little valley. This is a rather long but very easy zig-zag descent, apart from Dixcart Bay, the easiest in Sark.

The beach is safe for bathing,and offers a fine early morning swim when the tide is high. The bottom is somewhat bouldery after half-tide down and the sun leaves the bay fairly early. *[Excellent geological specimens of rock crystal and geodes can be found on this beach].*

The scramble is known as 'The Seven Caves' and starts by crossing the bay to a huge natural and detached arch; this is the Gull's Chapel — an extraordinarily fine piece of rock. Go through it and scramble up to a hole in the side of the cliff. This passage and all the following caves — with the exception of the Dog Cave — are free from the sea two hours each side of any low tide. At the end of this first tunnel on the right is a Fat Man's Misery: a small cave in which the larger members of a party are inserted in order to see if they are able to emerge through a hole in the top and descend again to the passage beneath; on the left, lying high in the rocks, is the small but exquisite Mercury's Pool.

Forwards from this a gully bends to the right and another small beach is discovered on the far side of which is a long tunnel terminating in a small jagged exit known as the Dragon's Teeth. Emerging on to a high rock platform another and larger bay is disclosed on the far side of which there are three caves which are worth exploring in detail.

The one farthest from the sea is of no consequence, the other two communicate via a high dark tunnel in which there is usually a pool. The height of this tunnel, which is under water at high tide, will give some idea of the tremendous tide rise in these islands.

Continuing round into the next bay we see a curious rock shaped like a knitting needle which is almost immediately below the Lighthouse on Point Robert, to its right is a cave with a shingle bottom and to the right again is a collapsed natural arch. The cave is longish and interesting in that it has an opening high up among huge, tumbled boulders.

Unless there is a low tide falling to 1.1 m. or less at least the return journey must be commenced at this point and the outward route retraced.

Rapid scramblers can reach The Dog Cave on a low tide of 1.1 m. as stated above; it takes about 20 minutes from this point and the cave must be reached before low tide as the water makes fast at the corner just before it. The going is easy but speed is essential. The Cave, which has long been thought inaccessible on foot and about which wild legends as to its depth have been repeated, lies at the head of a small bay on the Maseline side of Point Robert, just after one passes through a little rock gorge, and the harbor comes into view. It is at this point that the scrambler will be able to tell whether the time has been correctly judged, if so it is just possible to round the corner into the bay where the cave and its mouth will be dry and easily explored. Its total length is about 80 yards (75 m.) and there are a couple of interesting side shoots. Valette Bay, just round the next corner, is inaccessible except by swimming; the return to Greve de la Ville must, therefore, be made at once as the best part of an hour will be required.

Note: The Dog Cave is so named because it is said to "bark" at certain state of wind and tide.

THE HARBOURS AND LES LACHES

Excellent Bathing, good Fishing and a pleasant Walk.

Meeting a passenger boat is an unfailing amusement in Sark. A start should be made from the Collinette at about 10.15 a.m. to allow time for a visit to the old harbour — Le Creux. The roadway down past the Bel-Air with its overhanging trees and rippling water is the most picturesque in the Island, and in spring, when the hillsides are a mass of colour the walk is an especial pleasure. *[There is now a footpath which runs parallel to the road, alongside the stream, which is a delightful walk.]*

When the bottom is reached, one can first examine the two tunnels on the right which lead to the "Creux", the other on our left leads to the Maseline, which is visited later. The smaller and more ancient of these two tunnels was cut by Philippe de Carteret in Armada year ; it leads directly on to the little beach which, until a hundred years ago, was the principal landing place in Sark. Little imagination is needed to realise how impregnable the island must have been in the days of this one tunnel, barred, as we are told, "with two strong gates for its defence... and two pieces of ordnance above, always ready planted to prevent surprises."

The second and larger tunnel, cut in 1866 when the pier was constructed, has lost its original charm by reason of the concrete casing which rock fall made necessary in the 1920's.

The "Creux" is only used nowadays by the Guernsey boats if wind prevents a landing at the Maseline. Should the visitor be favoured by such an event he will be entranced at the seamanship required to tie up in this tiny port.

If the tide is high, and it must be remembered that this harbour dries out, there is no better way of spending a sunny morning than by lazily bathing in this beautiful basin of emerald water. It is the finest swimming bath in Sark. The surroundings are superb and there are usually a few small fishing boats and yachts to engage the attention. Les Laches landing lies to the right while the tide ripping between the Burons and the pier is in violent contrast to the placid waters within. Bathing here is excellent for swimmers and non-swimmers alike.

31

But first let us go to the Maseline Jetty and see a boat arrive. In high summer it will be full, and the 'Toast-rack' tractor-drawn buses will await the arrival of passengers on the landward side of the tunnel. On the quay tractors and trailers will be jostling for a place and for a short half-hour all will be bustle and animation. Bags are unloaded by all of the carters co-operating together, irrespective of their final destinations, a good example of Sark spirit!

Should it also be cargo boat day the unloading will take an hour or two, otherwise the crowds will disappear as quickly as they came though, and rod-and-line fishermen revert to their timeless occupation. Fishing at the Maseline and the "Creux" is good, especially for grey mullet, but most fish which frequent the Sark waters are taken here.

The Maseline Jetty was completed after the last war and declared open when the Island was visited by H.M. The Queen (then H.R.H. Princess Elizabeth) and the Duke of Edinburgh in 1949.

It provides deep-water facilities for the commercial vessels at all states of the tide and the days when passengers had to be ferried to Le Creux by rowing boat are gone for ever.

The walk back to the Collinette should be made over Les Laches Common.

Commencing the return journey up Harbour Hill take the first path on the left then cross the little stream and a short steep climb will bring us on to the cliff about 200ft (60 m.) above Creux Harbour with a fine view of Les Laches anchorage and the Burons rocks. In mid summer this is a common place to see the Bottlenose Dolphins which regularly visit the island. Follow the path at the top until in the S.W. corner of the Common a gate is reached from which a trackway winds back to Collinette past La Forge and the Peigneurie Cottages.

An alternative route up from the harbours is to take the path on the right, signed Cliff Path, as you begin to go up Harbour Hill. This ascends zig zag fashion and offers grand views over Maseline Harbour and The Grande Moie. Go through the gate at the end of the path. Bear left and the path opens on to a field. Walk along the left hand side of this and at the end turn right along the road. At the T junction bear left and after about 100 metres go through a gap in the hedge on your right. Continue between a group of modern houses then along a small road until you come to a T junction at which you bear left to return to La Collinette.

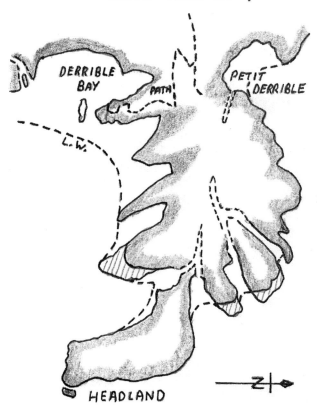

SKETCH PLAN No 4

DERRIBLE BAY

PETIT DERRIBLE

PATH

L.W.

HEADLAND

DERRIBLE BAY AND SURROUNDINGS

Fine sand Bay. Excellent Bathing. Remarkable rock scenery; a difficult Scramble through the Derrible Head Caverns.

There is a vast amount to be done in this area and a very early start must be made to gain a moderate idea of the district and even then repeated visits must be paid.

Leave la Collinette, passing the NatWest Bank, follow the road round to the left until some cottages (La Peigneurie) are reached, keep straight on past La Forge and just after a large semi-derelict building on the right at the top of the rise turn R through a gate and follow the field-hedge until the cliff is reached, then left along a footpath towards Derrible Head until the path to the bay will be seen 'zig-zagging' down. This path is a bit steep but steps have been cut where necessary. There is no danger in the descent and if the tide is half-way down the bay is easily reached; it is a particularly fine one and the beach is composed of sand. Under the facing cliff are some fine caves, two of which lead into the bottom of the Creux Derrible, the view of which upwards is even more impressive than from the top. It is said that the interior face of this Creux was once scaled by a foolhardy individual, but neither this or a climb up the outside are to be recommended.

The Hog's Back to the right is out of reach to scramblers, but Derrible Head — one of the finest pieces of rock scenery in Sark — is accessible at low tide.

"Derrible" is a very popular bay, the bathing is safe and there is ample room for the many parties who spend the day there. It is best to go in the morning of a falling tide as at high water the bay is entirely covered and one is forced back on to the rock platform at the foot of the path.

Those who are not interested in caves — and the scramble to the ones in the headland is not very easy — should make their way up by the same path, pausing at the top to take a view over Derrible Head and downwards into Petit Derrible Bay over the precipitous cliff known as Suicides' Leap.

34

The walk back to Collinette may be varied by taking the walk to the Hog's Back. Unfortunately, the old path to the top of the Derrible Creux is closed (2014) as the Island Authorities consider it to be hazardous. We do not comment! But splendid views of Derrible Head are obtained from the Hog's Back. One of the surviving Georgian cannon remains there, half buried, in the same position it was originally placed, all traces of its wooden gun-mount having long since rotted away. The path leads back along a field boundary until the Peigneurie Cottages and the spire of the NatWest bank render further direction unnecessary.

The Derrible Head Caves cannot be combined with a visit to the bay, time does not allow. They should be made the subject of a separate expedition. A low tide of at least 1.0 m. is essential and while it is possible for rapid scramblers to see the caves and return by the same route it must be emphasised that this is the only scramble described which can be said to be dangerous if attempted in its entirety without guidance.

Commencing from the rock platform at the foot of the path to the bay previously described, scramble southwards towards Derrible Head, making such progress as the tide permits — a start two hours before low tide is none too soon. It should be possible to cross the first beach and take lunch on the rocks before a halt is enforced and progress is barred. On again and across another beach gully we round a little point and descend to the beach in front of a large cave opening which should be entered as soon as it is wadeable. This excellent tunnel penetrates the neck of the headland and is shaped like a long-tailed chevron going deep in, of which one leg leads to a small rocky bay on the north of the point. Scrambling northwards and rounding another small promontory, another set of caves is reached and a similar pattern repeated on a larger scale, the second leg emerging into a deep gully the sea-end of which is wadeable; to the north again is another deep gully which can be entered at the top and left at its seaward end, but it is at this point, marked X on Sketch Plan No. 4, that a return by the same route is advised. Indeed, a return on this scramble should be made directly the tide turns, no matter what point the party has reached. On your return to Derrible Bay, you may be satisfied that you have seen a system which can easily rank with the more well-known Sark Caverns.

The Original Guide suggests a continuation to Petit Derrible, but this is not now possible due to severe cliff erosion at the back of the bay, and it can only be visited by kayak or dinghy from the Harbour.

Route No. 7   **Sketch Plan No. 5**

THE HOG'S BACK

One of the finest marine walks in Sark; steep descent to a good deep water Bathing and Fishing station. Interesting Caves.

Starting from Collinette as in Route 6, turn left at the Peigneurie Cottages and follow the path to the Hog's Back previously described, in reverse. Here, on each side, are splendid marine and pastoral views embracing Derrible Head, the Dixcart Valley and Bay and the whole of the coast southward as far as Breniere. The cannon on the headland is the starting-point for the descent and those who do not wish to essay this steep climb can vary their walk by returning until the Peigneurie Cottages can be seen and then break off left on the track down DixcartValley until Petit Dixcart is reached, where a right-hand path will take them up the valley (described under Route 8) to Stocks Hotel, where a spur path leads to the right up another open valley and on to the Rue du Moulin at the Manoir, turn right for Collinette which is five minutes' walk.

a) There is no mains water on Sark. All water is from wells, springs or from cisterns which collect water from the rooftops. This old gated well near Beauregard is typical of the wells used into the 21st century.

b) The Derrible Headland, pictured in 2014.

Plate V

(a)

(b)

The Evolution of La Coupée

The top left photograph shows the nature of the crossing between Sark and Little Sark as it was in the mid to late 1800s. The complete absence of handrails made crossing this narrow isthmus a very real danger with recorded fatalities in high winds. This led to the introduction of buttress and handrails in the first part of the walk, to save those emerging

Plate VI

(c)

(d)

from the relative shelter of the Sark-side gorge (b). In 1900 handrails were fitted to the entire length of La Coupée, no doubt appreciated by these fashionably dressed walkers of the period (c). Finally, after the Second World War the whole of the roadway was rebuilt in concrete (d) and much stronger handrails added by German prisoners of war working under the guidance of the Royal Engineers.

Plate VII

(a)

(b)

Grande Grève and the view over towards Little Sark (a) pictured in the 1930s and the natural arch at Dixcart Bay, (b) pictured in the early 1900s – neither view has changed significantly over the intervening time.

Plate VIII

The Headland and Caves.

Note: This expedition can only be undertaken on a grand maree — minimum for comfort, 0.7 m.

From the cannon, the cliff falls steeply to the point on the Dixcart side where a black rock ledge is visible from above.

Descend with care until a narrow path below an outcrop of rock skirts the edge of a deep inlet on its right and finally leads on to a rocky slope from which the ledge above described is easily reached. This is an excellent bathing and fishing place.

The gully on the Dixcart side which has just been passed at a higher level is the approach to one of the caves, but the best plan is to circle carefully in the opposite direction and to go round the point towards Derrible Bay until the second cave entrance is reached at the end of a steep gully opening towards Derrible Head.

It is here that the very lowest tide is needed if an awkward climb down, or a wade, is to be avoided - the lower the tide, the better!

The first section of the cave contains a long, very deep pool and leads round to the left into pitch-blackness, so a torch is vital. The floor dries out and eventually appears to end in a large smooth boulder (X on plan).

It is possible to negotiate a passage at the top of this rock and enter the cave which opens on to Dixcart Bay. This cave, although quite a long one, is usually dry and emerges on to a small beach from which it is an easy scramble back to the starting point. (It is impossible to scramble to Dixcart Bay from here).

For those who enjoy caves this can be an interesting and exciting excursion, but expect a wetting!

SKETCH PLAN No 5

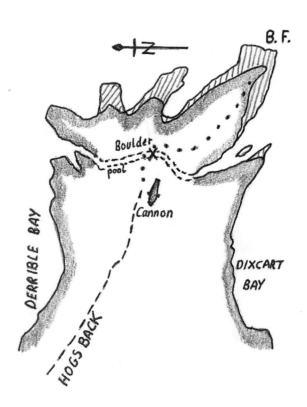

B.F.

Boulder

pool

Cannon

DERRIBLE BAY

HOGS BACK

DIXCART BAY

DIXCART BAY AND SURROUNDINGS

Most accessible *Beach* in Sark — safe *Bathing* at all tides — a splendid circular *Walk.*

Proceed from Collinette past the Nat West Bank, follow the road round to the left and then right by the Peigneurie Cottages and straight down Baker's Valley until reaching a footpath right, in front of the property 'Norwegian Wood' and skirting behind Petit Dixcart. Immediately beyond Petit Dixcart turn left down the Dixcart Valley path until the Bay is reached.

The return journey can embrace the whole of this beautiful valley by following the path back to Petit Dixcart and then proceeding straight on to Stocks Hotel as described in Route 7.

Dixcart Bay is the "Brighton" of Sark; it is of easy access, the bathing is off a shelving beach and safe at all tides, the surroundings are reassuringly beautiful albeit physically undemanding. The Natural Arch is justifiably famous and on the left or eastern side of the Bay behind an off-standing rock pinnacle is one of the longest caves in the Island. It can easily be reached on a spring tide and extends for some one hundred and fifteen metres under the Hog's Back; terminating in a small circular chamber. Because it bends almost at once, away from the light, the cave is dark for most of its length. It contains three long, deep pools and its exploration can be an eerie experience; the use of a good torch is advisable.

Dixcart Bay is particularly popular with young families. There is sand at low tide and plenty of space for recreation. For those who like a circular walk the cliff path to La Coupée is strongly recommended. Start back along the Dixcart Valley path and about 135 metres from its commencement take the ascending path to the left which is steep for a short distance and curves around below the grounds of La Jaspellerie. Approximately 100 metres beyond the entrance to La Jaspellerie where the track turns 90' to the right, there is a stile on the left hand side. Walking straight ahead with the fence on your left there is a small vineyard in a pretty hollow below. After 100 metres, there is another stile, and thus commences the footpath and from its switchbacks along the cliffs affording the most delightful views imaginable. The cliffs are high and the shoreline far beneath is almost inaccessible. It is a pity as there is much of interest beneath, including Dixcart Souffleur, the Pigeon Cave and finally Coupée Bay with the Cave of Laments on its southern flank. However, the enthusiast will no doubt find a local guide to show these marvels and meanwhile the pedestrian will eventually find himself on the trunk road of Sark a few metres from La Coupée (described under Route 15). The return to La Collinette is made by following the main road north to La Vauroque cross-roads, turn right there passing the Old Mill and Le Manoir, and finally along the length of the Avenue until the starting point is reached.

Route No. 9   **Sketch Plan No. 6**

THE POT TO ROUGE TERRIER

Mainly of interest to irrepressible scramblers. Good deep-water Bathing at Pignon and Rouge Terrier. Fishing at Pignon and Rouge Terrier.

Leave Collinette by the Avenue and Rue du Moulin, at La Vauroque crossroads turn left to La Coupee; cross it, pass the entrance to La Vermandee (house on cliff, right) and at next bungalow on the right turn left across a field until the cliff is reached, where the path will be easily found south of an old cider press. A certain amount of nerve is required for this climb; the Pot itself is fairly steep and being composed of loose earth and shale affords little or no hand or foot-hold. *[There is usually a rope provided here by volunteers, but use of the rope is entirely at the risk of the user]*. Before going down we will have a few minutes' rest and examine the view stretching before us. Away far to the south Jersey can easily be seen on a clear day — as can France to the east; further to the east is the south curve of Great Sark. The long rounded point to the eastward is Derrible Head, then Hog's Back, with Derrible Bay and Dixcart on either side.

Much of Little Sark cannot be seen, so let us now descend the Pot, using the rope as a 'steady' if required.

If we arrive well before low tide, it is interesting to have a quick look at the coast north of the Pot which is readily accessible as far as the great impassable gulley beneath Moie Fano. (See inset on Sketch Plan No. 6). The bathing in this area is not particularly good. Going northwards there are two smallish bays connected by a tunnel, in the second are a few caves of no great depth and in one a vein of the crystal known as Sark rock.

The stones in Sark are most interesting and few leave the Island without a few stones collected there. The best places are the two sides of the Coupee, Derrible and the Pot; Coupee Bay is far the best and will be more fully treated when we write of La Coupee.

However, time must not be wasted on this diversion as we should be on our way to Rouge Terrier directly the tide allows. This scramble can only be done on a very low tide at least 0.8 m. The cliffs are sheer, there is no way up until Pignon is reached and it is essentially a "scramblers" excursion as the difficulties are many and the scenic interest is slight; while for the able-bodied it is not too difficult in any sense of the word — it requires care and a certain amount of skill in rock climbing, which really lends the interest to the trip. There is very little rock reef, a great deal of wading through exceptionally long seaweed and the cliff has to be hugged nearly all the way.

Starting southwards from the Pot we come to a big dry gulley with a small cave at the end and shortly afterwards we come to another (the "Sweet Pea" cave) which extends right through the side of the cliff; this cave is indispensable to the journey and is invisible from sea and cliff. Inside there is always water but it is shallow. We emerge on to a small beach whence to the next headland the going is rather tricky, the cliffs come sheer to the water and to round the headland itself it is easiest to climb about 20 feet (6 m.) above water-level.

It is for the next piece of the climb, however, that the lowest tide is required, as it is only then that a ledge about two or three feet above the water's edge can be used. The water here is deep and this is the hardest part of the climb. However, in this climb, as in many others, although parts are only

SKETCH PLAN No. 6

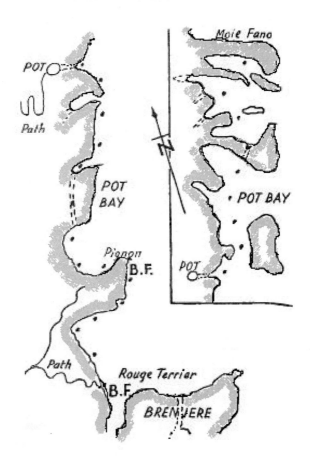

describable as difficult, there is no danger to life and limb, so long as the climber is a swimmer and not alone.

Here, for instance the worst penalty that a slip would incur would be a ducking in about twenty feet of water, and indeed such duckings are bound to occur now and again.

Once this section is encompassed, we have only to climb up on to the platform of Rouge Terrier.

This place is a good one for sitting and lunching, the rocks are flat and comfortable and the bathing at half-tide-up is very good indeed. The rocks at Pignon passed on the scramble can also be approached from the path up from Rouge Terrier and are an excellent place for bathing and fishing at almost any tide, although sadly this path is not always kept trimmed.

Down here at Rouge Terrier the current runs fast between the mainland and the Island of La Breniere, but at low water it is possible to walk across and explore this interesting islet and its natural arch.

When the time comes to return home the path leads up the cliff by long easy stages, passing through stiles and a field and then on to the "Gorey" roadway leading past the Moserie cottages and on to join the road to La Coupee at La Sablonnerie Hotel, returning to Collinette as on the outward journey.

Route No. 10   **See General Map**

ROUGE TERRIER TO VENUS POOL

Mainly of interest to Scramblers. Venus Pool—Bathing.

Note: While Venus Pool is fully described beneath, those who wish only to see this famous sight are referred to the direct and easy approach given under Route 11.

Descend to Rouge Terrier by the same route as that which we returned in Route 9. The rocks there are so delightful that it will be well to go about high tide and sit about there and bathe. The bathing there is excellent while the tide is fairly high.

When the tide is about half down we can start round to the south, through the gulley separating Breniere from the land. Boulders abound, but note the ancient wall (fort?) up on the right. We pass several small gulleys, small pools, and small caves, but there is little to delay us except the bad state of the going until we reach Venus Pool.

We have to choose between slippery seaweed and the crumbling rock of the cliff. This latter is most curious, and not at all satisfactory for climbing material; great chunks of it can be torn off in the hand.

Venus' Pool or Bath approached from this direction cannot be missed, while from the ordinary route it is distinctly hard to find for the first time. The pool is free from the sea about 2½ hours each side of low water so long as the sea is not rough, and is situated under a large overhanging rock, facing direct towards the Island of L'Etac (see map).

It is extremely beautiful, but while being more symmetrical than Adonis Pool (see Route 13) yet cannot approach the latter in attractiveness, whose very irregularities form a great part of its charms.

Nor are the seaweeds so beautiful in Venus' Bath, but we must not minimize the beauty of Venus, which is undeniable.

The Pool was about 18 feet (6 m.) deep and circular, but boulders at the bottom have reduced the depth. These rocks, clearly seen through the transparent water, are churned and churned by winter gales, becoming ever rounder and smoother.

A bathe here, of course, is inevitable, and inevitably delightful. From the east and south sides of the Pool excellent deep dives can be enjoyed.

If anyone is disappointed with this their first bathe in Venus, let them come again any fine sunny morning before 11 a.m., at which hour shade dispels the warm rays of the sun, and they will be enchanted with the spot. Close to is another large pool with a huge rock in the middle of it, and further a big gulley.

Our way home, however, lies along the vein of pale beige sandy rock which leads from Venus' Bath to the Path up the cliff.

The climb up the actual cliff is short, but very crumbling, and passes between two low cairns of piled rocks; we then branch off a little up the path through the ferns to the Silver Mines, and thence to the cottages of Little Sark where the road will be found to La Coupee and so home.

Route No. 11   **Sketch Plan No. 7**

THE COAST FROM VENUS POOL
TO PORT GOREY

Easily accessible coast; innumerable rock pools and sea gardens. Good "swimmers". Bathing at Venus' Pool, La Louge and Port Gorey.

At La Sablonnerie Hotel turn down left and up past the Moserie Cottages until you reach a metal gate on your right. Through the gate follow a broad grass track on to Gorey Common leaving the stone ventilation shafts of the old Silver Mines on the right. The path drops to a low shaley cliff top. Keeping L'Etac (see map) in front, daylight through the slit in Petit Etac can be seen. Keep this in view ; so long as this slit can be kept open, while descending the cliff we are going correctly. The descent should be made on the right side of the headland adjoining Clouet Bay, an easy descent along a sandy coloured vein of rock and when on the rocks follow around northward until Venus' Pool is found tucked under the headland on the Clouet Bay side. This fine rock pool was so named by the artist William Toplis, whose paintings of it are well-known. It is fully described under Route No. 10.

It is an easy and interesting scramble from here to La Louge, any low tide will do and the cliff can be regained almost anywhere before the Louge Tunnel, if desired.

All about "Venus" and for most part of the journey there are innumerable weed-fringed sea gardens and rock pools, great and small. Proceeding southwards we round a deep gulley to pass under the next headland, off which,

Path

CLOUET BAY

Venus
Pool

B

Jupiters
Pool

PLAT RUE BAY

Path

Gorey
Pool

B

Soufleur

LA LOUGE

N

46

about half an-hour each side of a spring tide, lies Jupiter's Pool, large and somewhat forbidding. Rounding the headland southwards we pass more pools and then crossing the mouth of Plat Roue Bay an interesting causeway leading up the cliff should be noticed. Its origin is said to be Roman. Crossing another gulley we come to a narrower one containing three caves, the largest of which is the Gorey Souffleur Cave. The pressure created by its domed roof throws, in a south-westerly gale, a column of spray to a considerable height. A little further on we come to an L-shaped gulley, which makes the outer rock an island and at the topof it a tunnel (the Louge tunnel) will be found. This leads through the headland, and contains a wadeable pool.

Emerging we are in La Louge, a deep and interesting inlet with a small cave, a sandy beach, and an old mine opening visible high up. The way out is up on to a rock platform on the northern side of the inlet and on it will be found another fine pool, Gorey Pool.

From here to Port Gorey is an easy climb for confident scramblers with a head for heights or a wade. *(Sadly it is not presently (2014) possible to go up at La Louge as the path is overgrown).*

Bathing at Port Gorey or at La Louge is good but best on a higher tide.

At Port Gorey we see the remains of the old Silver Mines with mine tailings and ruined buildings; these were started by Peter Le Pelley, the last Seigneur of that name, in 1835, who put all his savings into the workings. The venture was a failure, the Le Pelley family ruined and the Seigneurie subsequently passed into the hands of the present family. Sadly, the last remaining corner of the Engine House which stood as a grand landmark for many years, came down in the Valentine's Day gale of 2014. Lower down, a furnace and chimney still remain.

The mine trackway leads down to the landing-place, now disused, and up to join the road by which we went to Venus' Pool.

PORT GOREY TO ADONIS POOL
ROUGE CANEAU BAY

**A most interesting Bay containing numerous pools
and marine rock gardens. Bathing off rocks in
Port Gorey — approaching Adonis Pool the
hard way.**

(Note: Non-scramblers who wish to visit Rouge Caneau Bay: regrettably, at present (2014)the path down is overgrown. Time perhaps it was re-opened!?)

This climb is in many ways different to others in Sark, and therein lies a great part of its interest; there are none of the grand panoramas which abound elsewhere, nor do we pass through several bays, nor are there any of the great caves in this part. Our whole attention is confined to one bay and its two enclosing headlands, yet nonetheless this expedition is full of interest, and owing to various little difficulties it takes a whole tide to negotiate.

We go down to Port Gorey by passing through the metal gate (Route 1) and taking the descending path to the right. At a crossroads, turn right and follow the path round the inlet until a left turning. This leads to the cliff top and a descent to the western Port Gorey flats.

This place, as does the opposite side, affords an excellent bathe off the rocks, and while waiting for the tide to go down sufficiently for us to start, let us examine this inlet.

There is one small cave at the end of it, guarded at its entrance by a tall rock, whose top is fashioned in the shape of an eagle.

Adonis Pool, of course, lies round to the westward, so we must now get on our way. This first headland is rather a hard bit of climbing as there is a deep-water gulley which divides it from the island; the easiest way is to keep high up until the corner is rounded, and one can climb down into a long dry gulley.

SKETCH PLAN No. 8

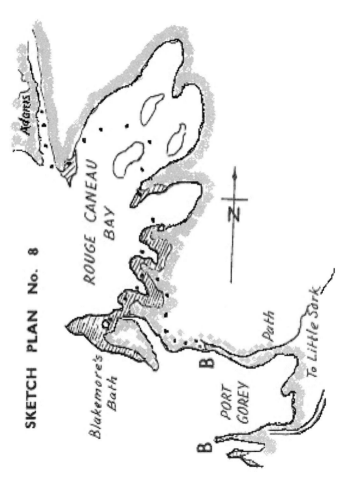

Addresses

ROUGE CANEAU BAY

N

Blakemore's Bath

PORT GOREY

B

B

Path

To Little Sark

We are now in Rouge Caneau Bay, which at a low part of the tide is absolutely infested with small islands and pools. The deep-water galley above referred to divides a rock — Moie — from the headland and on it there is a large rock basin known as Blakemore's Bath, approachable at low tide and in which a good bathe can be enjoyed. Otherwise, Rouge Caneau Bay does not offer good bathing; there is a small creek which gives a bathe at high tide.

These pools are so beautiful in shape and colour, so marvellously different from one another that a delightful hour or more can be well passed in exploring, bathing and probing to the utmost all these little marvels.

The lowest part of the tide is wanted for the rounding of the opposite headland out of the bay so we must not linger too long. It used to be possible to ascend out of Rouge Caneau, but the path is now dilapidated.

This is the hardest part we have to do on this trip, harder than the entrance to the bay. There is, however, at the worst, only the danger of a wetting. A low tide of at least 1.2 m. is essential.

The water, except at spring tides only, just goes down far enough to allow egress by wading, but it is not far before we can climb up above the water on to the cliff and so around to Adonis' Rock, just around the corner.

It is best to be frank, and for this bit over slippery rocks, with water all around about four feet deep, it may be said that the odds as to getting wet or not is an even-money chance —sometimes you slip and get wet, sometimes you don't.

For Adonis Pool and the way home thence, see Route No. 13.

(a)

(b)

A bathing party at Adonis pool (a), taken from the 1968 Fourth Edition, and (b)Venus pool on Little Sark as it is today.

Plate IX

(a)

(b)

Fontaine Creek in Little Sark (a) and Blakemore's Bath (b) both pictured in 2014. Blakemore's Bath was photographed by Jeremy La Trobe-Bateman retracing Route 12 for this book.

Plate X

ADONIS' POOL AND LES FONTAINES CREEK

Good Bathing: Adonis at low tide, Les Fontaines at high tide.

The Pool is, for a stranger, a distinctly difficult spot to discover, and so it will be well to explain the route at some length, after the Coupee has been passed.

From there continue along the one and only road in Little Sark as far as it goes, keeping straight on when the Sablonnerie Hotel is reached.

Then take the turning on the right by the last cottage, into the fields; the track then leads to the left for a time, disappearing into the gorse.

(Note: Those going direct to Les Fontaines Creek should strike more westerly, leaving a stone cottage on their right-hand, and entering a field gate, crossing the field down-hill when the path down will be quickly found as a gap in the hedge to the field; where the path forks, bear left for the Creek, as right is very steep and not without risk.)

From that point it is, for the first time, distinctly difficult for the stranger to find or for the guide to explain the route to the Pool.

All that can be said is that one must bear south-west, aiming for a point on the sea south of Guernsey and continue on to the most south-easterly headland.

Once there the visitor can easily see several landmarks to assist him. On the left as he looks southwards is the rock-strewn bay of Rouge Caneau; on his right is the long big island of Le Bretagne.

Between this island and the mainland he will see a large and detached rock, on the south of which glitters the Pool of Adonis two hundred feet below him.

The way down is just to his right and he will soon find himself on a wide ledge facing the rock on which the pool is situated.

51

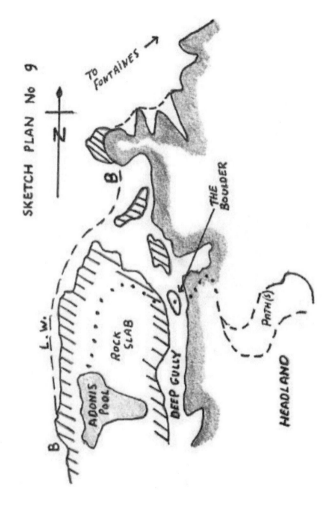

SKETCH PLAN No 9

N

TO FONTAINES →

B

THE BOULDER

B

L.W.

ADONIS POOL

ROCK SLAB

DEEP GULLY

PATH(S)

HEADLAND

52

Between him and his goal, however, there still yawns a deep gulley, which has yet to be negotiated; and the state of the tide makes a world of difference.

This deep gulley is dry about two hours each side of the average low tide, and it is crossed by means of a great boulder which stands in the middle of it. This crossing presents no difficulty to the able-bodied, provided an energetic person goes first and lends a hand with children and the less agile; thus the two gaps are easily negotiated.

The Pool cannot be mistaken and lies on the south end of the rock. In beauty, indeed in every respect, it far surpasses Venus' Bath or' any of the numerous other pools. It is from sixteen to eighteen feet in depth, and so transparent is the water that all the stones at the bottom can be clearly seen.

The Pool is lined with the softest and prettiest types of seaweed imaginable, and the surrounding rocks and pools all lend an additional beauty to the spot.

On all sides except the mainland side a plunge can be made into the pool with absolute safety. In short, no more delightful bathe can be imagined: it is the premier bathing place in Sark without a rival.

There are four other pools smaller in dimensions to one another on the rock.

Care should be taken that the return is made in time, as the tide comes up very fast, and the sea all around the rock is generally very rough and the current strong when the tide rises, often the sea rushes up and down the big gulley in an alarming manner.

When the tide is going down it is safe and easy to swim over to the big island opposite, and during spring tides it is even possible to walk over, although the bed of the sea is over 25 feet (7.50 m.) below the surface of the pool, thus the action of the tides can readily be imagined.

It is possible to scramble from Adonis Pool to Les Fontaines Gulley, the going is very difficult and not very rewarding, apart from a pleasant high tide bathe at Pequillon which can, in fact, be reached easily from above. (Care should be taken when bathing here at half-tide as there is considerable undertow).

Those who wish to go direct from Adonis Pool to Les Fontaines Creek should follow the cliff along until they reach the path referred to above. The descent is easy, and if the tide is halfway up the bathing is splendid, the gulley guarded to the north-west by Moie de la Fontaine is a natural swimming bath and certainly one of the best deep-water bathes in Sark. Non-swimmers can use it at low tide by an approach from Fontaine Bay (Route 14). The return both from Adonis Pool and Fontaine Creek is made by the outward route.

Route No. 14   **Sketch Plan No. 10**

LES FONTAINES BAY TO VERMANDEE BAY
(With an extension to La Grande Greve)

One of the best rock Scrambles on Sark. Good high-tide Bathing at Vermandee Bay.

This long scramble should only be attempted by quick climbers, and only be completed on a very low tide—falling to at least 0.6 m.

Proceed as in Route No. 13 as far as the cottages in Little Sark, and then instead of breaking towards Adonis Pool, keep straight on leaving a stone cottage on the right-hand, passing through a field gate, crossing a sloping meadow to the far hedge where a gap marks the start of the path down to the bay.

The start from Les Fontaines should be made as soon as the tide permits, and if the long journey to Grande Greve is particularly to be attempted, there is no time for dalliance as the arch at Pointe le Jeu must be reached before the tide turns. Start from Fontaines Bay (not the Creek) and cross the reef to the north, climbing above the high-water mark alongside the deep and interesting dry north-south gulley and descending there from to a narrow gulch in the rocks which is always at least knee deep in water. Follow this gulch along—wading is essential—until it drops to a small beach from which there is an inlet leading to a T-junction, both sections of which form a cul-de-sac. Examine this T and its small terminal caves but do not waste time trying to get out of it, the way is straight on past its entrance, and it is here that the first tide check usually occurs,

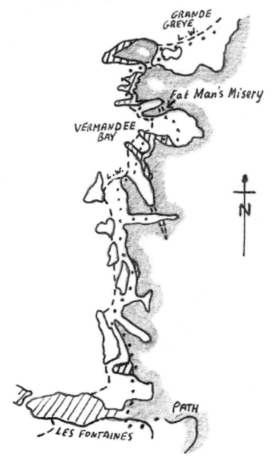

SKETCH PLAN No 10

GRANDE
GREVE
L.W.

Fat Man's Misery

VERMANDEE
BAY

L.W.

N

PATH

LES FONTAINES

55

and a short wait is necessary. Then, climbing above the tide mark once again, and dropping to another gulley, a great gash is finally reached on the right hand, up which is the way.

In this gash is one very interesting cave and others—they are known as the Black and White Caves—worth a visit. The way on is through a tunnel on the left hand about halfway up the gash which leads out to an exciting country of deep gulleys and tiny beaches, finally terminating in Vermandee Bay.

Head straight across the bay (those with time in hand can inspect a second fat man's misery—see plan) there are two more substantial reefs and gulleys to be crossed before finally descending a rock slide into the pool lying before the archway through Pointe le Jeu.

If the day is calm and the tide (0.6 m.) is dead low it should be possible to pass through it without falling in, but it is a fifty-fifty chance, and in any case the worst is then over. The remainder of the scramble to the path up from Grande Greve is easy going.

Route No. 15   **See General Map**

GRANDE GREVE AND LA COUPEE

Excellent sand beach and Bathing. Fine views and rock scenery. Good fishing for bass.

This is a delightful tour and one for which a bright day is wanted.

La Coupee is, of course, the sight *par excellence* of Sark; it is about 9ft. (3 m.) wide and a hundred yards (100 m.) long, while the precipices each side are about 100 m. from top to bottom.

If the visitor is a little disappointed with La Coupee, let him realise that it was not long ago there was no railing to give a semblance of protection and the passage was no more than a pony track. *[See Plates VI and VII-it is easy to see why children used to crawl over on their hands and knees in the winter gales!]*

Under these conditions the crossing might well cause a little awe at first, even 3 m. seems a small width with a 100 m. drop each side.

The view is very fine from here, there is always a fascination in gazing down great depths, away to the south is Jersey, and to the west is Guernsey and the Island of Brechou.

The Jersey side is impracticable, being almost sheer and composed of loose treacherous rocks: the ascent has been attempted but had to be abandoned.

There is a way down on the Big Sark side on to the rocks by the Convache Chasm. and so to the Coupee Bay, but this is dangerous and not to be recommended unless accompanied by a guide. The Convache Chasm is one of the finest pieces of scenery in Sark, and the colours in the cave are exceptional on a sunlit day. Coupee Bay explored by the same route has another interesting feature known as the Cave of Laments which is said to "groan" at a certain stage of the wind and tide.

The best, if not the only way, is to go by boat from Creux Harbour.

The Guernsey side, however, is quite practicable for anybody.

Pass through the railings on the Big Sark side of La Coupee and the path leads down by easy stages to La Grande Greve Bay, one of the loveliest in the islands, for the most part composed of firm sand with rocks here and there, the combination is beautiful beyond description. This path was built by volunteers when a large landslip in December 2009 swept over the previous one.

The bathing, of course, is grand and without danger except perhaps for the tide round Pointe du Joue, if one goes out too far.

This bay, the Coupee Bay and the Pot are the best places to find the stones for which Sark is famous.

Some valuable ones have been found, but they are rare; however, many of extreme beauty can be picked up if one is lucky.

Amethysts, emeralds, cat's eyes, crystals, agates, cornelians are all there in varying degrees of purity.

In the rough, of course, the stones take a little finding; the cat's eyes are best and, of course, the rarest; they are green-grey stones with a slight translucence round the edges. For the rest the others of value are generally transparent when held towards the sun.

Grande Greve is indeed a place in the sun, an ideal spot to be lazy in : the rocks on the left of the bay are very fine, so take some time to explore; there is a fine detached arch and two or three caves. To the northward of La Grande Greve lies the sandy bay of Port es Saies now, owing to a landslide, only accessible by a difficult scramble along the rocks from La Grande Greve. It is an interesting place with a long cave at its head in which there is a subterranean water-course. It is not possible to scramble from Port es Saies towards Havre Gosselin dry-shod, so the return must be made to La Grande Greve, and from there up the steps.

Route No. 16   **See General Map**

HAVRE GOSSELIN AND SURROUNDINGS

Good deep-water Bathing, Fishing. Nice walk.
Magnificent View.

This spot is perhaps the easiest of all to find, for anyone who has been to Sark only for a day must have seen the Pilcher Monument situated on the headland called the Longue Pointe, the most westerly portion of Sark facing Brechou Island and Guernsey.

From the Collinette pass through the Avenue, past the Manor and the Mill, until the crossroads at La Vaurocque are reached. Keep straight on, passing a pond and a picturesque stone house on the right-hand side. Follow the road left, then right keeping on the track on the high ground until the Pilcher Monument—a granite pinnacle—is seen about 200 yards (180 m.) ahead. This stern monument was erected in memory of a Mr. Pilcher and his companions who perished in a storm in 1868. It is stated that Mr. Pitcher over-ruled his companions' fears on setting out for Guernsey—they were never seen again. Many visitors think that the view from this eminence surpasses all others in Sark (even that from Eperquerie Common along the west coast of the Island).

Behind us lie the green undulations of Big Sark, on our right the Gouliot Caves'southern entrances; next the Moie de Gouliot between which and the Island of Brechou the Gouliot Race foams and tears. The grand Beleme Cliff on Brechou (now a private island) and behind are Jethou, Herm and Guernsey forming the background to this rewarding view.

Immediately below us the zig-zag path leads down to the old landing ladder and the new breakwater, where there are more fine rocks, with their foamy rings; so clear is the water that the cables of anchored boats and shoals of fish can be distinguished far below the surface. Turning southwards, a fresh panorama stretches before us, revealing all of the west coast of Little Sark from La Grande Greve to La Moie de Bretagne, but before passing on we must mention the little islands which lie off La Pointe de Jeu, Les Baveuses, they are only about 22 feet (7 m.) above average low-water and are covered at high water; their interest lies in the noise the sea makes over them as the tide rises and falls from which they earn their name—'The Slobberers'.

The headland immediately in front of us is the Longue Pointe, beneath, and in its southern flank lies the Victor Hugo Cave, perhaps the most renowned cavern in Sark, occasioned perhaps by a magnificent entrance and a legend of impenetrable depth. It is not, in fact, very long—some 35 m.—and at the end there is a small shaft emerging into a gulley facing southwards from which further progress is impossible except by swimming. It is unwise to attempt to visit the "Hugo" without a guide, the area is dangerous and there have been fatalities in recent years; in any case, it can only be entered by boat or by swimming and there is, at times, a nasty undertow as also at the next Moie south—Les Orgeries.

Now let us go down the path to the Harbour. At the last bend on the right an offshoot leads to the old ladder landing—the only means of access before the jetty was built; a hair-raising experience for the unaccustomed. The ladder is considered unsafe at present (2014). The Harbour itself is a good place to spend the day bathing, picnicking, and fishing. The steps make easy the non-divers' descent to water, and when the sun moves round, the reef to the left, provides good bathing facilities at all tides.

The little bay—Telegraph Bay which lies to the right of the ladder, can be reached by a path from Fregondee. Sadly, its use is discouraged by the landlord these days, as it is a charming spot when the afternoon sun is on it. The telegraph cable to Guernsey from which it was named is now disused.

Route No. 17   **Sketch Plan. No. 11**

THE GOULIOT CAVES

Famous Caverns. — Pleasant Walk.

The visit to the Gouliot Caves is one of the best of all, the caves are so grand, so weird, and so fascinating, while the very difficulty in reaching them makes it seem that the views there gained are snatched, as it were, from them in the very teeth of the ocean. The inner passages of the caves can only be visited during the spring tides that come round with the new or full moons. On a calm day a low tide of at least 1.1 m. is sufficient to see the inner caves.

It will be useful to remember that spring tide low always occurs at early afternoon and high six and a half hours later.

Starting from La Vaurocque, thence keep straight on to the pond and Le Petit Beauregard, as in Route 16, but turning right round the house through a white gate, following the track sharp left past a bungalow until the common is reached. (This land is private, but the owner raises no objection to the use of the path provided gates are shut and the sheep are not disturbed; dogs are not allowed because of this).

Follow the broad grass path as it descends towards the headland, and at the neck just before the rocky part is reached a footpath will be seen falling away to the right and following along the top of a sea gorge. It, too, runs out to the edge of a little rocky promontory, and here one turns to the left across a sloping shoulder of rock where the worn foot-track will be seen.

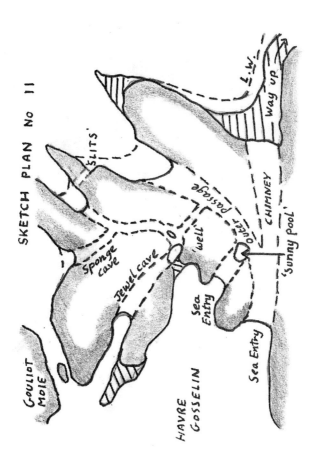

SKETCH PLAN No 11

L.W.

Way up

'SLITS'

Passage

CHIMNEY

Sponge cave

Jewel cave

Well

Outer

'Sunny Pool'

Sea Entry

GOULIOT Mole

HAVRE GOSSELIN

Sea Entry

61

In a few paces the "chimney" entrance to the caves will be found and the descent into the main cavern commenced. This chimney and the huge fine cave which it leads into can always be visited at any low tide, and are well worth a visit in themselves.

At the bottom of the chimney the view is magnificent; behind, the sky can he seen up the chimney just traversed. In front there are two large entrances, and another round to the right, while the magnificent roof is held up by pillars and arches like those of a great cathedral.

The opening most to the left affords us a pretty view of Havre Gosselin, the ladder, and above, the Pitcher Monument. This, as many other views in the cave, makes a fine photograph.

The next opening to the contains the "Sunny Pool" and a sea entrance. Here strong swimmers might prefer to visit the rest of the caves, but, as the water is deep, we will pursue our way along the cave to the right.

On our way again there is an opening on the left, "The Well", dark and narrow with chest-deep water in it. This leads direct into the inner caves, but again we will go to the end of our passage, which brings us out on to a beach below the opening to the chimney.

So far we have done nothing impossible at any low tide, but we have only been waiting for the actual lowest part of our spring tide, for the other caves can only be visited during the lowest half-hour dry shod.

The way in lies under the little split arch, known as the Slits, on the left as we face the sea and then again round to the left is the entrance to all the rest of the caves, the Anemone and the others. The caves are found to divide later, one leading to the dark narrow tunnel into the main cave already mentioned, while that on the right—the Jewel Cave—leads out to the sea.

To describe these inner caves with any justice is very difficult, and where other far more eminent and qualified people have only partly succeeded, the authors must crave the reader's indulgence.

The walls from top to bottom and the roof are simply a *mass* of anemones: red, pink, green and white, glistening with the water which has only just left them.

(a)

(b)

A group of happy cave scramblers pictured in the Mouton Cave (a) and a family exploring Inner Gouliot (b), both taken from the 1968 Fourth Edition.

Plate XI

(a)

(b)

Port du Moulin (a) and Les Autelets (b) pictured in the 1930s, and remarkably unchanged today.

Plate XII

Here there are species which are normally only found in deeper water, thanks to the unique nature of these passages and the strong tidal flows - they form a perpetual delight to all lovers of natural history and botany, as do also the little sponges that appear wherever the anemones leave them room. *(Divers who swim through these caves when full tell us that they are even more spectacular when in "full bloom").*

We must now hurry back to make room for our friend—the tide. There is good deep-water bathing at the point of the sea gorge we followed down, but the final descent to the rock slab needs care, so caution is called for, and this puts many people off.

Those who do not wish to descend to the caves will find the headland above a very agreeable place for reading and picnicking, and if the broad path across the common is followed until the trail leads to the left, a rewarding detour round the cliffs can be made, rejoining the Gouliot path at the first gate on the common.

Route No. 18   **See General Map**

LA SEIGNEURIE AND LE PORT DU MOULIN

Seigneurie Gardens. Cliff walks.
Good beach bathing.

Port du Moulin is the jumping-off place for two first-class scrambling excursions described separately under Routes 19 and 20, but the bay itself and its surroundings offer sufficient to justify a separate descriptive section.

Start down the Avenue turning right to the Church at the Gallery Stores and Post Office, passing the Church, the old Hall and the Chief Pleas Assembly room on the right, to the Clos a Jaon crossroads, then straight on until the main Seigneurie gates are seen on the left. The gardens are open every day, and are well worth a visit. At the end of the Seigneurie Wall take a track turning left, this ends in a path above the grey stone cottages of L'Ecluse. Port du Moulin beach is well signposted; but before taking the turning down a short but fine cliff walk leads straight on to the cliffs above and further round to a view of Saignie Bay. The views here of the west coast and north end are some of the finest in Sark.

Returning, follow the path downward until a level platform is reached, from which it drops left-handed and crosses a stream. Again, before descending further, walk to the end of the flat area, examine the "Window in the Rock " cut in the sheer cliff face overlooking Port du Moulin, and the fine view of the natural arch it affords.

There is another small promenade which is well worth making. After crossing the stream above referred to and continuing along the downward path, a branch will be seen ascending to the left-hand side of the valley, and this, if followed to its limit, enables the visitor to reach the headland immediately facing Tintageu with a fine view of the Moie de Mouton, the Gouliot Passage and Brechou. Here is an excellent place for a quiet day reading and picnicking.

Going back to the path down to the bay, it passes a little waterfall where the stream from the Seigneurie fishponds cascades to the beach and Port du Moulin is finally reached.

This is a very popular bay, the beach bathing is safe and when the tide is high, very pleasant. When the tide goes down it leaves the natural arch at its northern end free, through which a more secluded bathing gulley will be found. This area, as far as the Autelets, has many good pools and the remains of a shipwreck. Further on Saignie Bay gives good sand bathing at low tide, but remember the sole means of retreat is through the natural arch and a close eye must be kept on the time and tide rise.

The scramblers' way on from Saignie is described under Route 20, and that at the south end under Route 19, but it should be noted that Port du Moulin in itself can well account for a day's excursion.

MOULIN TO MOUTON

A good scramble and a fine cave. Sand bathing
at low tide.

Contrary to the normal procedure, this route is described in an anti-clockwise direction because the Moie de Mouton Cave (at the end of the journey) must be reached at low tide. For those who wish to see the cave or bathe at Port a la Jument, the direct way to that bay is given at the end of this synopsis.

It should be said that while there is no danger in this scramble, there are two difficult points en route, which are more easily overcome if the party includes two or three agile men, as rather high obstacles have to be surmounted. A low tide of at least 1.1 m. is desirable.

From the foot of the Port du Moulin path we head off into Pegane Bay between Tintageu and the main island. There is an interesting cave in this bay which we can explore while waiting for the time to make possible an approach to the next little headland, which has to be climbed over (and here an agile pair of scramblers are a great help to the party). The next bit requires some care and skill as a deep gulley has to be traversed and somewhat uncertain wading through others in deep water has to be completed before the next little headland is reached, not so high as the last, but smooth without handholds, and again a pair of strong men are an asset.

That done the sand at Port a la Jument is reached without much trouble. Waste no time, but keep straight across the bay and clamber round the side of the Moie de Mouton, where a deep gulley with a low cave entrance at its end will be found. On a low tide of at least 1.0 m. this gulley can be entered from the sea end, otherwise a descent into it, with a little trial and error, or a short rope, can be made close to the cliff by the cave entrance. This is the back entrance to the Mouton Cave. At ordinary spring tides it is accessible for half-an-hour or so each side of low water by wading. Torches are necessary, as almost immediately on entry the cave turns right, narrows and enters a dark tunnel in which there is a knee-deep pool, from which one ascends and

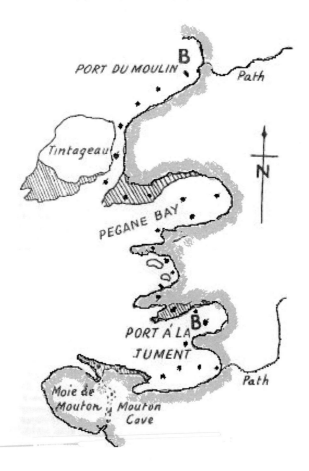

emerges into the dramatic square-roofed Mouton Cave, leading us right through the Moie to the southern side. It is no exaggeration to say that as a single cave, it would be hard to find its equal in interest and splendour.

It is impossible to go out of the southern entrance and around the Moie to our starting point, but before retracing our steps to Jument Bay, we should spend a minute or two watching the sea birds, this is is a favourite nesting place.

Back again in Jument Bay we can rest, bathe and picnic. The spectacular path up lies behind us, and skirting around to the right of an old farmstead, passing two delightful houses and their gardens, enters the Rue du Sermon just by the Chapel and the old graveyard (see Map 12).

Route No. 20   **Sketch Plan No. 13**

SAIGNIE BAY TO LE PLATON

A fine scramble. Bathing and fishing at Le Platon.

Proceed to the Natural Arch in Port du Moulin as in Route No. 18. This excellent scramble, which traverses the coast known as Les Sept Moies can only be attempted on a low tide of at least 0.6 m.; it is one of the longest of Sark scrambles and well worth doing.But be prepared for rough country and maybe a wetting! There is a great deal to see, and as the difficult part is nearly at the end, the earliest possible start should be made and passage through the natural arch at the north end of Port du Moulin effected as soon as it is wade-able.

The going from this point to Saignie Bay is over rocks large and small, passing between the Autelets and the cliff. Push on as fast as the tide permits, to the far side of Saignie noting the Souffleur Cave (operational in a westerly swell) and enter the cave in the little point just beyond it. This has a convenient branch tunnel which makes the next gulley accessible, and here, in order to gain time, it is necessary to clamber over the rock reef on the right to gain the next bay and the carafe-shaped inlet beyond. At the top of its neck part will be found a very narrow crevice through which it is just possible to crawl.

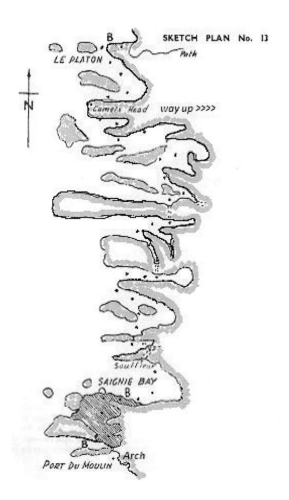

SKETCH PLAN No. 13

B

LE PLATON

Path

N

Camels Head

way up >>>>

Souffleur

SAIGNIE BAY

B

B

Arch

PORT DU MOULIN

This leads to a long gulley which in turn debouches into another, but narrower, inlet from which another similar cleft makes further progress possible. Indeed, without these two privy passages the journey could not be made.

This latter chink leads to a confused archipelago of rock islands traversed by deep gulleys. Immediately to the right of its northern end there is a small cave, but waste no time in exploration as the trickiest part is to come.

Follow straight on, keeping as near to the cliff as possible, when the easily recognisable low headland, colloquially known as the Camel's Head will be seen, and it is the ascent of the rocks at the foot of this promontory which calls for the lowest point of tide as the last gulley is deep and the seaweed particularly treacherous; late comers are sure to get wet at this point. If it is found impossible to reach this place there is an easy way up as shown on the Sketch Plan. The Camel's Head can also be easily ascended up an earthy green chimney on its north side, once over the obvious first difficulty.

However, there is still another bouldery bay to cross before Le Platon is reached, and this challenging scramble is done. From the black rocks of Le Platon a path leads up to a small headland, from which the cliff top is easily, if steeply reached; by the cannon which lies at the end of Eperquerie Common. This is a fine scramble, one of the best in Sark, but no time must be lost on the journey.

Route 21   **General map**

Round the Island in a Boat

(In the Latrobes' day, passing around the island in a boat was done in a rowing or small sail boat, with the requisite pair of sturdy boatmen. It took the best part of a day, and luncheon was part of the experience as described in the text that follows.

George Guille has for many years taken people around the island in his trusty boat, the 'Non Pareil', (see Fig. b) and the trip now takes only around 2 ½-3 hours, lunch no longer being needed. George has kindly updated the original text factually, but otherwise it remains unaltered).

'This is a delightful trip which can be recommended for all types of visitors and especially for those who for some reason or other are unable to climb up and down the cliffs, as they can, by this means, get a good idea of what their more fortunate friends can do, and what they cannot do, such as the Convache and Pigeon Caves, which we go by. Parties are made up through the hotels and guest houses whenever the weather is suitable. The start is usually made from Creux Harbour and the direction depends upon which way the tide is flowing. For the purposes of this description it is assumed that the flow is northward and that we set off in that direction, passing the Buron Rocks.

The first point of interest reached is Dog Cave (see page 28) just short of Point Robert, and very nearly under the Lighthouse, which we pass by: the cave derives its name from the action of the sea at a certain state of the tide when it makes a noise like a dog barking.

The Lighthouse was finished in October, 1913, and the light was first used early in 1914.

After Point Robert, we pass round into Greve de la Ville Bay with its splendid succession of caves which reach right from the Gulls' Chapel, in the south-west corner of the beach, to Point Robert itself (Route 4).

Passing the Banquette landing (see Route 3) and rounding Banquette Point, we pass the Red Cave (see Route 2) or Cave of the Drinking Horse, which is best seen at half-tide, when the resemblance is marked. This is a tall narrow cave which only just allows the entrance of a very small dinghy or boat, too narrow for today's boats.

Passing Les Fontaines Bay containing Creux Belet, the Fern Cave, and the Fairy Grotto (see Route 2), the Eperquerie Landing is reached, and finally the three rock islands of the north end—La Grune, Le Corbee du Nez and the Bec du Nez. A very strong tide runs round the "North End" and then whirls away to Herm and Jethou.

The next object of interest is the Boutique Caves (see Route 1). One entrance can be seen just south of La Grune, and we soon come to the main sea entrance, and the sheer gulley leading down to the "chimney" described in Route No. 1. On a high tide, we may enter this main sea entrance.

The coast from here onwards is known as Les Sept Moies, on account of the seven detached rock headlands which lie between the Boutiques and

70

Saignie Bay, and is extremely interesting and more fully described in Route 20. Note the curious and rather beautiful isolated rock standing off Le Platon with a top like a Bishop's Mitre, also known as 'Queen Victoria', and the headland shaped like and named, a Camel's Head.

At the commencement of Saignie Bay notice the Souffleur Cave, second on the left, which works in a north-westerly gale, and those fine off-standing rocks known as the Autelets ahead. Often entry to the adjacent cave is possible.

Crossing Port du Moulin, where the Moie Tintageu is seen at its best, we head for the Moie de Mouton lying at the south end of Port a la Jument and fully described under Route 19. The "back" entrance of the cave can often be entered before we float in at the main southern end. This surely is the finest sea cave in Sark with its dramatic flat roof and brilliantly coloured walls. It is interesting to note that the low tide entrance gulley described in Route 19 is now well below the bottom of our boat.

All round the Moie is a great place for all varieties of local sea birds, especially Shags, Fulmars and Peregrine Falcons.

Before lunch we have one more cavern — a great one in the eastern point of Brechou — and the Gouliot Passage to run, passing in the process the Gouliot Caves described in Route No. 17. They cannot be entered in a boat. Luncheon nowadays is usually taken at Havre Gosselin, the party being allowed about one hour ashore *(as the trip is now short enough for lunch to be omitted, no longer, sadly!)*. Almost immediately after re-embarking, we turn, if conditions permit. into the spectacular Victor Hugo Cave (see Route No. 16).

(a) Leslie la Trobe Foster (right) leaving the Creux Harbour with his family and 2 boatmen.

Hugo reputedly named it. He spent some time on Sark gathering material for The Toilers of the Sea. *(To enter this cave, it has to be a flat-calm sea, George only managed it 7 times in the 2014 season)* For many years it was thought that this cave was of great depth. This is not so; the conjecture was probably caused by the difficulty of access. *(George reports that the cave IS actually very high and deep, approx. 50 meters).*

We have now done with the big caves until passing the south end of the Island, but there is much to look at en route.

First, it is of interest to look into Port es Saies, now, owing to a landslide, impossible to access from above. The cave at its head contains a fine stream of fresh water. Crossing Grande Greve, the height of La Coupee can be more fully appreciated. Pointe le Joue, with its tunnelled headland, Vermandee Bay and the coast from there to Les Fontaines described in Route No. 14 all command our interest until the famous Adonis Pool (Route No. 13) is reached.

Then on round the south end passing Rouge Caneau Bay, Port Gorey and entering the narrow rock-strewn passage between the main island and L'Etac de Sark. *(The deep sea passage here is no wider than a road.)*

L'Etac is alive with sea birds, especially puffins and gulls, landing is difficult, and the cave referred to by John Oxenham in "Maid of the Silver Sea" is an author's fiction. Le Petit Etac, lying north of the main rock, has a natural arch.

On our left is the Gorey Souffleur Cave (see Route 11) and a little farther on Venus' Pool lies coyly under a bluff of granite not easy to detect from the sea.

Clouet Bay and Brenniere Bay are of no great interest, but the little Cromlech lying on the cliff of the former should be noted, as also the fine rock of Brenniere with its great natural tunnel which we now approach.

The coast from this point on to Coupee Bay is described under Route No. 9: Rouge Terrier and Pignon Landings, the long cliff tunnel which makes its traverse possible, the Pot and lastly Moie Fano, that "misplaced" headland so reminiscent of Lear's drawings of Corfu that one wonders if Ansted did not name it.

And then we are at Coupee Bay, on the left the Cave of Laments and on the right the Convache Chasm which we enter, a fine cave with beautiful natural lighting. Adjacent is the Pigeon Cave, some 140 yards (125 m.) in length — the longest on the island (see page 38). The colour of the rocks is a pinky grey which seems to have suggested the name. There is another very long and beautiful cave, which has no name, a few yards north of the Pigeon, its roof is so low that it cannot be entered by boat, and it is completely drowned at high tide. The rocks in this case are like green marble, quite different from the Pigeon. A little further on before Noir Bec we shall see, if the tide allows, some part of the Dixcart Souffleur Cave, and should there be a slight swell from the south-east, it may give some evidence of its action.

We next make for Point Derrible, crossing Dixcart Bay and Derrible Bay with fine views of the Hog's Back and the interesting headland of Derrible, all the entrances to caves described in Route 6 can be identified. The Brown Cave and the Cathedral Cave are the last items on our route, which takes us on past the Platon a Moie around Les Laches to the starting point of Creux Harbour.

Given a good day, this is a most worthwhile excursion. Luncheon should always be taken, and liquid refreshment for the boatmen is seldom unappreciated.' *(a sentiment which the modern day boatmen, including the one pictured below, would no doubt heartily endorse!)*

(b)

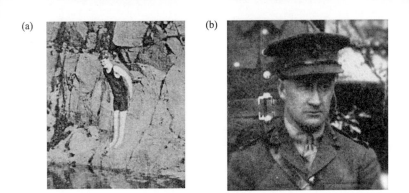

(a)   (b)

The 'Latrobes'.
Geoffrey (a) pictured about to dive into the Adonis pool, and (b) later, in obviously less care-free days. Leslie is pictured in Route 21 (Fig. a).

(c)

The boy's mother, Amy La Trobe Foster (c) descending Port a la Jument, in the 1913 equivalent of hiking apparel, with one of her sons in the background.

Plate XIII

Biographical Note

Who were the 'Latrobes'?

Although using the *nom de plume* of 'the Latrobes', the Sark guide was written by two young brothers, Geoffrey and Leslie La Trobe Foster. They were the children of a barrister from Eccles in Lancashire, Arthur La Trobe Foster and his wife Amy Constance Carter. The family had moved from Lancashire to Dover on Arthur's retirement. The boys spent three successive holidays on the Island of Sark between 1911 and 1913 with their mother. They would have been 15 and 19 respectively on their first visit and were clearly keen explorers of the Sark coastline.

In the late Victorian era, hiking and scrambling in the countryside became very popular. The boys would almost certainly have had access to a previous work on the outdoor exploration of Sark, 'Scrambles in Sark' which was published in 1861 by W.B.Woolnough. When they published their own guide in 1914, Leslie would have been 23 and Geoffrey 18, and this comes across in the freshness and charm of the prose. The book was printed just as the world was about to change forever, with the outbreak of the Great War. Both brothers signed up for the military service, Leslie in November 1914. He served as a Lieutenant in the Royal Marines. Geoffrey signed up in 1916, became a Second Lieutenant in the Royal Fusiliers, was wounded in February 1917 and demobilized in 1920. Both brothers survived the war. Lesley served for a second time in the Royal Marines in the Second World War, and died in 1952. Geoffrey, became a teacher, later becoming headmaster of the Bow School, Durham, and lived to the ripe old age of 88, dying in 1984 in Claro, north Yorkshire.

The fact that both boys would have gone straight from publishing this account of their carefree exploration of their own idyllic island paradise, to the horrors of the First World War in the space of a few short months, lends this text an intense poignancy and which resonates still today, a hundred years later.

Acknowledgements

We are indebted to all those before us who have seen the need to resuscitate the La Trobe guide over the years. We have based this Centenary edition heavily on the Sixth edition, published in 1980 by The Guernsey Press Co. Ltd. We hope that by making this version a 'not-for-profit' enterprise, with all proceeds donated to the Professor Saint Medical Trust on Sark, if we have infringed any copyright, we will be forgiven.

We thank Michelle Wilson for patience and skill in scanning much of the original content in order to produce an editable copy, Ruth Waugh for typing the extra material, and Dr Mark Holmes for scanning the old photographs. Dinah Bott of the Priaulx Library, Guernsey researched the lives of the Latrobe brothers with great skill, Jeanne Razzell gave I.T. advice, and Jan Wade advice on publishing, and all are gratefully thanked.

We thank Kimberley Hatch, Printing Newmarket, for her good humour, patience and skill, given in equal measure, in guiding this project to completion.

Sark Island Hotels kindly supplied a map of the new footpaths around La Moinerie for inclusion on the large map.

All of the routes were re-walked by volunteers in 2014, so that amendments could be made. Thankfully Sark has by and large survived intact, with perhaps more significant changes to the island happening in the last 5 years than in the previous 95. There were in consequence relatively few changes, but we sincerely thanks those who gave up their time to re walk the routes.

They are listed below, in route order:

Route	1-2	**Jeremy la Trobe Bateman**
Route	3	**Rob and Lynn Pilsworth**
Route	4	**Jeremy la Trobe Bateman**
Route	5	**Jan Guy**
Route	6-7	**Jeremy la Trobe Bateman**
Route	8	**Paul and Jane Armorgie**
Routes	9-20	**Jeremy la Trobe Bateman**
Route	21	**George Guille**

Picture Credits

The Photographs in this Guide have been drawn from several sources, outlined below, and the editors are very grateful for permission to use them, where applicable.

Antique Postcards
Plate II (a), VI (a) and (b), Plate VII (d), Plate VIII (b).

Antique Souvenir pack: '12 Beautiful Views of Sark' – date unknown, probably 1930's
Plate I (a), Plate IV (a) , Plate VIII (a), Plate XII (a) and (b).

Guide to the Coast, Caves and Bays of Sark, (4th Edition) , Guernsey
Press Co Ltd, (1968) Plate I (b), Plate II (c), Plate III (a), Plate V (a), Plate IX (a), Plate XI (a)

Guide to Sark (2nd Edition), G and L Latrobe, Tozers Printers, Guernsey, (1914)
Frontispiece (a), Route 21, Fig. (a), Plate XIII (a) and (c).

From the editors private collections
Frontispiece (b) and (c), Plate II (b), Plate III (b), Plate IV (b), Plate V (b), Plate IX (b), Plate X (a) and (b).

Sue Daly
Plate I (c)

The Bow, Durham School.
'A Centenary Record, 1885-1985', Plate VIII (b)

Michelle Perrée - www.simplysark.co.uk
Route 21, Fig. (b)

Karen Adams, Sark Tourism Office
Guille advertisement picture

Andy Stobbie, Guernsey
Gallery Stores advertisement picture

Stocks Hotel

LOCATED IN THE HEART OF THE PICTURESQUE DIXCART VALLEY

(Route 8 in this guide)

Originally built as a working farm in 1741, Stocks continues to afford discerning guests the luxury of every conceivable modern amenity including comfortable beds, electrical lighting, and both hot & cold running water, piped directly to your room!

Hearty breakfasts, wholesome lunches and romantic candlelit dinners are served daily (at individual tables!).

Local lobster and crab are a speciality.

Today, the hotel remains proudly in local family ownership and is personally managed by Paul Armorgie, with a team of discreetly efficient and professional staff.

The finest traditions of island hospitality are blended with the luxury of contemporary creature comforts.
In short Stocks remains a destination to satisfy *all* of your Sark desires.
email reception@stockshotel.com
Interweb: www.stockshotel.com

Telephone **01481 832001**